Reckless opportunists

Manchester University Press

The *Manchester Capitalism* book series

General Editor

MICK MORAN

Manchester Capitalism is a series of books which follows the trail of money and power across the systems of our failing capitalism. The books make powerful interventions about who gets what and why in a research-based and solidly argued way that is accessible for the concerned citizen. They go beyond critique of neoliberalism and its satellite knowledges to re-frame our problems and offer solutions about what is to be done.

Manchester was the city of Engels and Free Trade where the twin philosophies of collectivism and free market liberalism were elaborated. It is now the home of this venture in radical thinking that challenges self-serving elites. We see the provincial radicalism rooted here as the ideal place from which to cast a cold light on the big issues of economic renewal, financial reform and political mobilisation.

Already published:

The end of the experiment?: From competition to the foundational economy

Licensed larceny: Infrastructure, financial extraction and the global South

What a Waste: Outsourcing and how it goes wrong

The econocracy: The perils of leaving economics to the experts

Forthcoming:

Safe as houses: Private greed, political negligence and housing policy after Grenfell

Foundational economy: The infrastructure of everyday life

Systems city: A new politics of provision for an urbanized planet

Our academic editors are Julie Froud and Mick Moran. Our commissioning editors at MUP are Tom Dark and Tony Mason.

Praise for *Reckless opportunists*

'Aeron Davis has spent two decades talking to members of the financial, political, and media elites – and here he lines them all up to explain how they've created the debacle that is Brexit Britain. The company boss says he may himself be sacked at any moment. The prize-winning journalist worries over why he hasn't got the story everyone else apparently has. And the law-maker admits he hasn't a clue about the laws he's passing. And the only thing stopping them carrying on like this forever is bad luck – or a better democracy.'
Aditya Chakrabortty, Senior Economics Commentator, *The Guardian*

'Aeron Davis pulls back the curtain on the wizards of Oz who rule us. And having studied them for decades he tells their story brilliantly. They were never as good as we were led to believe. Leadership doesn't have to be solitary, rich, nasty, brutish and short. It can be connected, modestly-paid, nice, civilized and long. And that would be pretty beneficial to everyone else too.'
Danny Dorling, Professor of Geography at the University of Oxford

'An indispensable addition to elite scholarship that was decades in the making and arrives not a minute too soon. As the West continues to quake in the face of "populist" furore, Aeron Davis's deft analysis of his "barbarians inside the gate" shows an establishment torn asunder. Confounding past assumptions of both the left and right, Davis weaves the reader through the top corridors of U.K. power, and finds an elite that is "precarious, rootless and increasingly self-serving." Scholars and pundits trying to make sense of the establishment overthrow in the West will ignore *Reckless opportunists* at their own peril.'
Janine. R. Wedel, author of *Unaccountable: How the Establishment Corrupted Our Finances, Freedom, and Politics and Created an Outsider Class* and University Professor in the Schar School of Policy and Government, George Mason University

'Aeron Davis's new book on the Establishment re-writes the rules of the genre. He is a rare thing, a critical outsider who has managed to gain extensive insider access. His close-up accounts offer fascinating new insights into the apparent dysfunction of modern politics and sometimes the dysfunctionality of modern day politicians.'
Iain Dale, political commentator, publisher, LBC broadcaster

'Chaos often feels like the best word to describe the world my generation is inheriting. *Reckless opportunists* shines a light on how the decay of the Establishment feeds that chaos. It's terrifying but it also gives me hope that a different and better world is possible.'
Joe Earle, co-author of *The econocracy*

Reckless opportunists

Elites at the end of the Establishment

Aeron Davis

Manchester University Press

Published by Manchester University Press
Altrincham Street, Manchester M1 7JA
www.manchesteruniversitypress.co.uk

British Library Cataloguing-in-Publication Data
A catalogue record for this book is available from the British Library

ISBN 978 1 5261 2727 3 hardback

ISBN 978 1 5261 2728 0 paperback

First published 2018

Typeset
by Toppan Best-set Premedia Limited
Printed in Great Britain
by Bell & Bain Ltd, Glasgow

Contents

Acknowledgements

This book was written over a summer but was twenty years in the making. So there have been many people to thank over that time.

First of all, I am very grateful to those 350 individuals who agreed to talk to me through the years. Many were extremely generous with their time and forthcoming with their accounts. I have many vivid memories of the good, the bad and the unusual.

Some of those moments that have stuck in my mind longer include: spending a whole afternoon listening to Neil Kinnock's stories of the '80s in a greasy spoon over endless cups of tea and most of a packet of fags; Michael White's account of his punch-up with Alastair Campbell (and hearing Campbell's version some time later); listening to David Bailey's potted history of the City which explained the 2007 financial crash better than any book I've read; Mark Wilson's blockbuster story of international boardroom intrigues at a large financial corporation in the wake of that crash; Iain Duncan Smith's Pythonesque attempts to appear busy and important; Dennis Skinner's foul-mouthed soundbites and Ann Widdecombe's down-to-earth charm; an extended semiotics lesson from Tim Jackaman on what the financial pages of the *FT* really mean; Polly Toynbee's acute observations of how political personalities and policy-making interact; Paul Staines' loud denunciation of elites and socialists alike over a pint in an empty pub; Sir John Gieve's warts-and-all social history of life in the Treasury; and Jeremy Corbyn turning up at my sixth-floor office with his bike for an interview.

Second, I want to mention some of those who have been advisors and supporters at different points while working on related projects. They include: Peter van Aelst, Olivier Baisnee, Rod Benson, Clea Bourne, Aditya Chakrabortty, Rosemary Crompton, James Curran, Kelly Davis, Will Dinan, Bob Franklin, Des Freedman, Peter Golding,

Jonathan Hardy, Gholam Khiabany, Roman Krznaric, Colin Leys, Andrew McGettigan, David Miller, Liz Moor, Ann Pettifor, Angela Phillips, Mike Savage, Bill Schwarz, Bev Skeggs, Chris Taylor, Grahame Thompson, John Thompson, Peter Thompson, Daya Thussu and Dwayne Winseck.

Then there are those who have had a particular input on elites and this book. They include: Philip Augar, Andrew Bowman, Roger Burrows, Will Davies, Danny Dorling, Ewald Engelen, Ismail Erturk, Julie Froud, Charles Harvey, Dan Hind, Sukhdev Johal, Anu Kantola, Adam Leaver, Bong-hyun Lee, Joris Luyendijk, Mairi Maclean, Tom Mills, Mark Mizruchi, Catherine Walsh and Janine Wedel.

Jamie Keenan has produced a wonderful cover design. Many thanks are due to Chris Hart and all the production team at MUP. I owe a great debt to Tom Dark, Mick Moran and Karel Williams who persuaded me to write the book. Karel, in particular, is relentless when it comes to corralling academics into doing more useful things with their research time. All three checked in regularly with me during the writing process, and read and commented on the manuscript. And, last of all, my close family: Anne, Hannah, Miriam and Kezia. They put up with me being chained to the desk over a long, hot summer, when I could have been enjoying picnics and ball sports in the park instead.

Introduction

As I write this introduction, the British elite appear to be weaving from one full-blown crisis to the next. They have splintered in many directions. The Conservatives admit austerity hasn't worked out but they have no plan B. Debt and market bubbles are inflating again. The country is several months into its negotiations with the EU over the terms of Brexit, but no-one, including Theresa May and her Cabinet, has any idea of what they are negotiating for; nor what is best for the Tory Party, let alone the country.

Many see this as just another low point in the cycle of Establishment control. The vote for Brexit profoundly shocked many of those in charge. But still, at some point, they will get their act together. They did after Suez in 1956, the IMF bailout in 1976, and the ERM[1] debacle in 1992. Britain will become great again, even if that greatness will be mainly reserved for a small group at the top.

The problem is that Brexit was not a recent one-off. Scarcely anyone grasped how disastrous US-UK policy in the Middle East and Central Asia after 2001 would prove. The elite also failed to see the rapid rise of Scottish nationalism in 2014, or that the Conservatives would lose their majority in 2017. No-one foresaw the scale of the financial crash in 2000, or the one in 2007–8, or the one coming to a high street near you soon.

I would argue that these multiple crises are no coincidence. Neither can they be put down to the actions of a few deficient personalities. It is a structural problem that has developed over decades. The great transformations of the 1980s onwards have not only upended societies, they have reshaped leadership itself. Globalisation, turbo capitalism, financial engineering and new communication technologies have destabilised and disoriented elites as much as anyone else.

This has produced a new generation of leaders who are struggling to maintain some form of command. Regardless of intent, they lack expertise and vision. They are precarious, rootless and increasingly self-serving. Although many have done exceptionally well in material terms, their ability to shape events and influence perceptions is in steep decline. And they have yet to come to terms with the economic and political gulf between themselves and the rest of the population.

My sense of this evolving long-term crisis has become clearer after many years of speaking to those at the top. Often when talking to leaders, I have suddenly understood that they are not in control. I'm aware that I'm talking to someone plugged into power, money or both; someone who knows where their interests lie. But they are not really in charge.

I got that strong impression when talking to Baron Alistair Darling about his time as Chancellor of the Exchequer. Darling, by his own account, wasn't supposed to be in charge when the great financial crisis hit: 'I was there really as what Brown saw as a temporary thing.' He wasn't an economist, just a 'safe pair of hands'. He was keeping the seat warm for Gordon Brown's chosen successor Ed Balls. Then the banking system began to collapse. He was left managing potential financial Armageddon with all the control of a novice rider holding on to a bolting stallion.

The late Lord Cecil Parkinson, by his own admission, was surprised to find himself a senior cabinet minister. 'Not the brightest tool in the box' said one of his former cabinet colleagues. He is now better remembered for fathering an illegitimate child and having his career cut short, yet he was the politician who pushed through 'Big Bang' in 1983 (the changes happened two years later). This deregulated the financial sector and had a profound and lasting effect on the UK economy. Parkinson had somehow achieved this, secretly outmanoeuvring the Cabinet and City Establishment in a matter of a few weeks. As he confided in me, it had to be quick because he knew the news of his extra-marital affair would soon become public.

I had a similar feeling when David Nish told me about his first experience of being at the top. Nish was riding high at Scottish Power, a FTSE 100 company: 'People thought of me as the next Chief Executive of Scottish Power. I was very successful.' And then: 'I came in on a Monday morning and the Chief Executive said to me "David, I want you to go".' Sir Michael Davis was another to grab defeat from the jaws of victory. He seemed to be at the top of his game, leading a merger to create the biggest mining company in the world. Things suddenly went sour overnight, and he was ejected just as the deal was being signed off.

It's these moments that have given rise to this book because they don't quite fit the characterisations of elites and the Establishment as they are constructed by both left and right. For the Establishment itself, as with the classic elite theorists writing a century ago,[2] leaders are in control because they are superior. They are knowledgeable, innovative, visionary, hard-working, charismatic, self-made and many other things. They got to the top on merit and because they were winners amongst winners. They drag the nation along with them towards prosperity and are richly rewarded accordingly.

For the left, like the critical elite theorists writing in the post-war period,[3] it is about control based on power rather than innate ability. Those on top are privileged, socially cohesive and able to shape events to secure their shared, collective interests. Whether impeding innovation or driving change they adapt to ensure their status quo prevails. And the Establishment always wins.

However, there is an alternative view put here, which is that the modern generation of leaders are neither expert nor visionary; nor are they socially cohesive or in control. Too many are just reckless opportunists making the best of what they have amid the chaos they have helped to create. That's how people might characterise the likes of Boris Johnson and Michael Gove, Fred Goodwin and Philip Green, Rebekah Brooks and Richard Desmond, and several others besides.

Yes, they can earn more than ever before and their decisions have powerful consequences that are widely felt. They are highly skilled when it comes to pursuing their self-interest. But, they are also rather less able to influence public opinion or predict the consequences of their actions. What is best for them can often be bad for their organisation, their employees or publics. Their failings are not only damaging the wider public, economy and society, they are undermining the very foundations of elite rule itself.

This leaves a series of questions to be answered. First off, how did we end up systematically producing the leaders that got us here? How do they get to the top and how do they survive once there? How do they cope with the lack of power that everyone assumes they have? And, how do they get out, personal fortunes and reputations intact, before anyone notices the damage they have caused?

This book attempts to answer these questions by offering a more intimate view of the everyday working lives of leaders in Britain. It is based on 20 years of researching elite figures in five areas associated with the modern Establishment: the national media, the City, large corporations, the Whitehall civil service and the major political parties at Westminster. Over that time, I have interviewed and observed over 350 people working in or close to the top.

One thing that has become apparent to me is that, although the professional worlds that these varied leaders inhabit are different, they also contain many parallels. The ways elites are selected, constrained and incentivised everywhere has meant we are producing a generation of self-serving, insecure and less competent leaders. They have the abilities and skill sets needed *to become* leaders but not those required *to be* good leaders. They are always on the move and can't afford to invest meaningfully in personal relations or in gaining expert knowledge.

Once in power, they are inward-looking, creating their own cultures and are cut off from their publics. They stay there, insulated from criticism and protected through institutional impenetrability. They are rewarded for creating and gaming their own evaluation systems. They succeed by making short-term gains and pushing larger, long-term problems into the future. And, when things fall apart they run to the safety of the pack, or they up sticks and move on. For the cunning leader, there is always another business, institution or country to relocate to and screw up.

This book departs from convention in two obvious ways. For one, although this is a close-up, fly-on-the-wall style account, it is also very much an outsider's perspective. Most detailed and personal studies of the British Establishment have been produced by those who have a certain familiarity with their subject. Their authors had a privileged education, they became Oxbridge dons or joined the national media. Many ended up with a title and in the House of Lords. I didn't and won't. The social history I have produced here is more that of the middle-brow, sociologist interloper.

The down-side to this is that I have not always got the level and depth of access that others have obtained. On the plus side, it also means I don't have to worry about bumping into my subjects each day and can be a bit more ill-mannered. I also get to start sentences with 'And' and cannot resort to boring you with my Classics knowledge.

The second difference is in the way the book is organised. Almost every other study of elites or the Establishment explores the topic sector by sector, as if constructing a national map of power marked out by distinct elite professions. This one mixes up all five of my sectors in each chapter. This is because, for me, it is the many similarities of disparate elites and institutions that are so interesting.

Leaders are more alike than different in the ways they develop personal strategies, make risk assessments, relate to systems and ideas, look at their peers, and respond to fashions. The dilemmas and constraints of leadership have many parallels and operate in the same self-destructive ways. It is the similarities and their consequences that I am keen to reveal here.

And although the book is based on five elite sectors in Britain, I feel that many of the issues and similarities discussed are more universal across the top tiers. Whenever I give a talk on these issues, inevitably people come up and tell me how it describes their experiences of leaders in other occupations and countries.

The book is organised in four parts. Part I surveys the elite state of play in Britain as it is now. Chapter 1 argues that the Establishment, as it has been conceived, is coming to an end. Chapter 2 looks at how elites, by trying to get ahead, have destabilised the very institutions on which their power is based.

Part II looks at how leaders have adapted to get to the top. Those most suited to pleasing their assessors get there first. That means PPE degrees and MBAs[4] rather than qualifications in law or engineering; media management and accounting skills instead of creativity and entrepreneurship. Sellers now trump makers, and bluffers outrank experts.

Part III reveals some of the ways elites stay at the top once they get there. As Chapter 5 shows, joining the club means sharing its culture and ideas, and adopting dominant norms and positions, no matter how nonsensical. Chapter 6 looks at the secrets and lies that underpin elite power and control. Some are systematic and organised, and some are simply the lies leaders tell themselves. Chapter 7 shows that leadership has been transformed into a numbers game because numbers can be tallied up in a way that ideas can't. And because elites co-create the game, they can also change the rules as and when they need to.

Part IV focuses on exit strategies and how canny elites survive when it all goes wrong. As Chapter 8 shows, leaders follow far more than they lead. It's safer that way. And when the going gets tough, the tough join the herd. Chapter 9 is all about mobility, because the modern leader must be ready to up and go whenever things start falling apart. Staying ahead no longer means staying on top of one organisation or nation but floating across several.

The final conclusion tries to join the dots and briefly explores what solutions there might be to the current problems of leadership.

Notes

1 IMF: International Monetary Fund; ERM: Exchange Rate Mechanism.
2 See the classic elite accounts of Vilfredo Pareto and Gaetano Mosca.
3 See the work of C. Wright Mills, in particular his (1956) *The Power Elite*, Oxford: Oxford University Press; or one of G. William Domhoff's many editions of *Who Rules America?*
4 PPE: Philosophy, Politics and Economics; MBA: Master of Business Administration.

Part I

BARBARIANS INSIDE THE GATE

1 The end of the Establishment?

Introduction

In 2014, Owen Jones's *The Establishment*[1] explained how and why Britain's unequal, class-ridden system would always prevail. It was written at a time when the elite seemed to be thriving in spite of recently writing off the global economy. After a couple of lean years for Davos man, bank debt had effectively been nationalised. No-one in power had had to go to jail. Self-enrichment for the few was going better than ever.

As Jones explained, the Establishment had reinvented itself, with new players and ideas. It was now as dominant as ever. For many, there has always been an Establishment – a socially coherent body working towards its own collective interests and managing Britain accordingly. Accounts of the Establishment vary considerably but they all agree that there is one.

Developments since then have sorely tested that assumption. In 2016, the British Establishment was thrown into disarray once again, when the UK voted to leave the European Union. David Cameron and George Osborne, the victors of the 2015 election, were suddenly cast adrift. Boris Johnson and Michael Gove, the leaders of the successful leave campaign, having stabbed Cameron in the back, then stabbed each other. The now broken party of the Establishment was dragging the country towards financial ruin and endangering the future of the Union.

Meanwhile, the Bank of England and captains of industry found themselves wondering who and what to support. Their political party, the only one they had ever championed was following a course of action they thought would wreck the economy. Stirling and the FTSE 100 index plummeted. Shareholders began revolting and bankers relocating.

A year later, the Establishment seemed to be recovering once again. Theresa May, without a vote, had been quickly installed as Prime Minister. Cameron's old Etonian chumocracy may have been shoved out but fox-hunting, low taxes and austerity, selective schools, nationalism and imperial trading ambitions were all on the agenda. The right-wing press, unchallenged by a pliant BBC, were demolishing what was left of Jeremy Corbyn's Labour Party.

And then came the snap June 2017 election. The Conservatives, with all their resources and an initial 20-point poll lead, lost their majority. Theresa May was outperformed by a badly dressed, pacifist republican with no money, no media support and a shadow cabinet that could fit in a phone box (although admirably supported by hundreds of thousands of ordinary members). The Tory Party was left negotiating a Brexit deal with a dead duck leader, a hung Parliament, and no idea of what outcomes the Establishment wanted.

All of which suggests that it might be time to question whether the British Establishment still functions. Yes, some members of the elite have become very rich. They are united in their fear and loathing of left-wing ideas and ordinary publics. Their decisions have powerful consequences that are widely felt. But they are also rather less able to exert control or predict what those consequences will be. As a body, they have reached a tipping point. They are no longer coherent or collective or competent. These failings are not only causing larger schisms, inequalities and precariousness in Britain; they also threaten the very foundations of Establishment rule itself.

The Establishment: reinvention or decline?

The Establishment has been changing for as long as the term has been in public use. Many, on both left and right, prefer to think of the transformations as reinvention rather than decline. But, arguably, it's more the other way around. This is because many of the traditional elements that once held the Establishment together are degenerating, with little to replace them. We have new elites but not a new Establishment.

It was A.J.P. Taylor and Henry Fairlie[2] who brought the term to popular attention in published sketches in the 1950s. But it was Hugh Thomas and Anthony Sampson[3] who filled in the details – the who and the how. These accounts documented an elite network.

Those in the network had power, status, privilege and money, and they looked after their own. The male-dominated history of the Establishment was intertwined with that of the monarchy, aristocracy and landed gentry.

Its members went to one of seven 'Clarendon' public schools like Eton, Rugby or Harrow.[4] They moved on to Sandhurst or an Oxbridge college. They then glided effortlessly into a variety of powerful positions in private or public organisations. Political control operated through the great state institutions of the Church of England, Westminster, Whitehall and the armed forces. The economy was a stitch-up, coordinated through a public-private partnership of the Treasury, Bank of England, the City and business leaders. The BBC and national press ensured that 'the common people' accepted this state of affairs.

These elites reproduced and maintained their collective identity via exclusive social circuits. These included membership of expensive London clubs with names like the Garrick and Athenaeum. If they hadn't already inherited a title, they would get one soon enough, ending their days in that gilded care home (or finishing school) known as the House of Lords.

Much changed through the decades. The documenters of the Establishment recorded new developments with each new generation. Older elite sectors declined and new ones took their place. In accounts written in the 1990s by Jeremy Paxman, Andrew Adonis and Stephen Pollard,[5] the power and influence of the Church, monarchy, aristocracy and army had clearly waned. Sampson's final *Anatomy of Britain*,[6] in 2004, records the stark decline of many Victorian-era institutions, and the power grabs made by new, abrasive business types and unassimilated foreigners.

But these authors also identified continuities. Old institutions, starting with the Clarendon-Oxbridge conveyor belt, seemed to operate as smoothly as ever. That sense of shared elite interests, acting across private and public networks, and protecting one's own, endured. Inequalities continued to grow. Owen Jones's 2014 sense of outrage about today's Establishment is as strong as A.J.P. Taylor's and Henry Fairlie's back in the 1950s (although their source of outrage was different).

Arguably, what these authors described as elite reinvention and renewal was only partially right. Underneath, there was a more fundamental, long-term weakening taking place of the social foundations and institutions of power. Some of these have appeared now to fracture beyond repair. This isn't just a matter of a new Establishment replacing an old one.

This started to become clear to me when recently researching those at the top of both the civil service and business world. Interviews with former career mandarins revealed just how much Whitehall had changed. The service they had joined in the 1960s and 1970s was the preserve of the Establishment amateur. The large majority had come from Oxbridge, having previously studied history, classics or something else that failed to equip them for managing an archaic state bureaucracy. Generalists ruled and specialists occupied the lower rungs.

As Sir Alan Budd explained, in relation to the Treasury, the department was not run by professional economists. Instead, those in charge deferred to the 'Brown Book', a government tome explaining how to use certain technical levers to respond to shifts in employment, inflation, etc. It was sort of a *Dummies Guide* to managing the British economy: 'if you wanted to, say, reduce unemployment by 100,000, there were various ways of doing this ... it was very like say if you opened any textbook, like sums, any textbook anyone read at university. The chapter on macroeconomics, this explained how you did things'.

As Lord Turnbull, the former head of the civil service, recalled, the economic shocks of the 1970s and the political ones of the 1980s set in motion real change. From his account, it became clear that even the British Establishment had realised it could no longer afford to be managed by privileged amateurs. 'Meritocracy' and expertise, represented by grammar school education, the professions and PhDs, began dictating the new recruitment policy:

> and gradually the classics people, the humanities people slowly got replaced. We used to have people who were experts when I arrived, on Byron, and musicians. Rather refined people. Then, rather hard-nosed economists gradually took over and the dominant culture became not music, but football and golf as the kind of cultural shift.

Sir John Gieve reflected on the culls that took place somewhere between the 1976 financial crisis and the early years of Mrs Thatcher's first term in office: 'everyone was called Douglas, I seem to remember when I arrived at the Treasury, and most of them left.' The two top layers of the Treasury were removed. Instead, a relatively junior member, who 'was willing to challenge the orthodoxy and wasn't a typical smoothy', was elevated up to the top of the department.

I had begun recording a similar shift in corporate management in the 1990s. A telling example of the change taking place was the takeover of the exclusive Trust House Forte hotel chain by Granada Media in 1995. The story typified the declining power of the old Establishment. Sir Rocco Forte led the hotel group. He was son of Lord Forte, regularly donated to the Conservative Party, and entertained the ranks of the elite at his country estate. As everyone remembered, he had been out shooting grouse on the moors when the takeover bid was announced.

Gerry Robinson, who drove home the hostile bid, came from a poor Irish family and had become a dynamic new force in the corporate world. When he had earlier managed to capture Granada, John Cleese had called him 'an upstart caterer cunt'. That had only improved his standing in the City. Both the press coverage and many people involved felt this narrative dominated everything. Flabby, inefficient old money was being run out of town by a new energetic breed succeeding on merit. Chris Hopson, who headed up the Granada communications team, explained the symbolism of it all:

> The shooting thing was, in fact, a perfect analogy for our views and claims about how Forte was running the business. It summed up a company that was being run as a series of trophy hotels, that was an archaic family business, that wasted time on pomp and ceremony. So, it was a perfect analogy and it fell into our hands – too good to resist.

This changing leadership profile was all the more pronounced talking to 30 of the UK's top business leaders nearly two decades later. Only a third of those interviewed came from a wealthy, upper-class background or had attended a public school. None had gone to one of the elite Clarendon schools. Only 3 of the 30 had both a private education and had graduated from an Oxbridge college. Several came from poor immigrant families without a trace of C of E. Only a couple really registered as blue-blood Establishment by the measures first set out by Thomas and Sampson.

Some wore chunky gold jewellery and had fake tans. People like Paul Walsh (Diageo), Gareth Davis (Imperial Tobacco) and Alan

Parker (Whitbread) sounded decidedly gruff. Few liked to draw attention to any elements of privilege in their education or upbringing. They got to where they had on a mix of merit and luck. Some proudly brandished their outsider status, sounding quite anti-Establishment.

One of these was Andrew Owens, the founder and CEO of Greenergy, a fuel distribution business. It's a company most people have never heard of, but it's been listed as one the UK's top two largest private companies by turnover for several years now. Owens's father was a school caretaker and his mother a school cook. He says his own school was one of the worst in Britain: 'they set the bar low and they fell over it pissed on a Friday night. All they really cared about was beating Cardiff High in rugby.'

Owens is a tough ducker and diver, always on the move. He doesn't have his own office but hot desks with his laptop as he moves from base to base. Asked about the reasons for his success, he says he is 'fiercely tribal' when it comes to his own people and employees but to no-one and nothing else. He puts his achievements down to being quicker, more ruthless and more hard-headed than the big FTSE companies and soft management that runs them. Who knows what John Cleese would have called him? The word that does come up several times is 'disruptive':

> I don't give a shit about losing, that's about it really. I do not associate anything I do with my personal self-image. I don't go along thinking I'm diminished as an individual. So, I don't care about failure really … my own point differentiation is clear when I deal with people from bigger companies. It's just that I'm more fearless than them and therefore I find it very simple to take decisions that other people can't take … so, we've been a disruptive technology in an area where people think you can't be disruptive.

Owens is ready to condemn slow, privileged types everywhere – in big business, in the financial sector, politicians and government. Like many CEOs, especially those in private companies, he is critical of the 'broken' London Stock Exchange. And, like others, he is even more critical of politicians. But his most scathing comments are reserved for the civil service:

> Whitehall is full of absolute idiots. It's become a self-fulfilling black hole of hope. It's just full of young somethings with a double first

from Oxford, piling in over industrial policy ... it blocks anything happening, because anything gets put into a decision matrix non-activity fest. It's shameful ... this idea that you can get civil servants who are paid a fraction of the money that you could earn in industry, somehow making better judgements than industry. It's nonsense.

These changing leadership demographics and opinions were not just particular to those leaders I talked to. Anthony Sampson's 1962 account captured a civil service that was changing but one still dominated by those with a private education and a classics degree; 87% had been recruited from a handful of Oxbridge colleges. So, too, older studies of business leaders reveal a Clarendon-Oxbridge past. One study of top company chairmen in the 1970s showed that two thirds of them went to a private school, with over half overall attending a Clarendon one; 85% of those who went to university (a third didn't go) ended up at Oxbridge.[7]

Leap forward several decades and things have changed considerably. Peter Barberis's[8] study of civil service mandarins from the 1830s onwards reveals the long-term steady decline of such demographic profiles. A 2014 study[9] revealed that just over half of permanent secretaries had been to private school and a similar proportion to Oxbridge. Only 22% of FTSE 350 CEOs had a private education and 18% went to Oxbridge (just 12% of those on the *Sunday Times* Rich List). The senior judiciary and armed forces are still clearly dominated by those with such an educational background. But in most other elite sectors, the figures are more like a third or less.

The interviews and longer-term survey data reveal a couple of important trends. First, there has been a shift in elite power from public to private since the 1950s. This is a strong feature of the Establishment literature that emerges in the wake of the Thatcher revolution. For Jeremy Paxman, the new 'radical Toryism' was nearly as brutal towards the old Establishment as it was to industrialised labour. In so doing, it had created 'another elite, a new monied caste'.

For Andrew Adonis and Stephen Pollard, a 'super class' of highly paid professionals has formed in law, accountancy and other sectors. This has produced a new 'closely interlocked cadre', separating itself from the rest. They, along with Robert Peston,[10] writing in the wake of the 2007–8 financial crisis, have no doubt where real wealth and power have gravitated: the City of London and its networks stretching out across the global financial system. These days a third to a half of FTSE 100 companies are led by non-British chief executives. The majority of shares are no longer owned by UK individuals or their pension funds but are traded by large, unattached international investors.

Second, the automatic links between exclusive education, tradition, status, power and money, which once typified the Establishment, have been broken. A far smaller percentage of those in power have taken the Clarendon-Oxbridge conveyor belt to the top. Exclusive London clubs lie empty or, worse still for elites, now allow women, foreigners and lower-class members to join. The members of the aristocracy, once liberally sprinkled across the boards of public institutions and corporations alike, have vanished from sight.

Many of those in the corporate and financial worlds have a less elite education and privileged past but a lot more money and influence. Those working at the top of state institutions are more likely to be of good Establishment stock, and to receive honours, but also to have less income and questionable influence.

This has left the various parts of the current Establishment more disparate and more antagonistic towards each other. Dame Margaret Beckett witnessed this growing fragmentation, both in political opposition and government:

> I remember John Smith gave a talk in the City at one point, reasonably close to the 1992 election, and it was almost like the bride's side and groom's side. There were the people from the financial world who were there, and there were the people from the industrial world who were there. And they almost kind of weren't talking to each other, and literally almost sitting on different sides of the room with different interests and concerns … civil servants, on the whole, even the best ones, hated you to be taking advice from people outside. One of my colleagues almost refused to see anybody from industry about anything in case he was thought to have compromised himself in any way.

With the educational and cultural links eroded, so too the shared values associated with the old Establishment are disappearing. Earlier accounts observed that 'public service' was a noble aspiration of the elite. National pride was a value shared across its different parts; one that could always unite an otherwise class-divided society. As George Orwell noted in 1941, however useless the upper classes were, they believed in service to the nation: 'One thing that has always shown that the English ruling class are morally fairly sound, is that in time of war they are ready enough to get themselves killed.'[11]

Such a sense of national duty and self-sacrifice is decidedly absent in the new elite. Instead, the values of those at the top are all about 'personal enrichment', 'individualism', 'enlightened self-interest' and a reverence for the 'wealth creators'. But such norms are antithetical to any sense of shared, collective interests. Selfish individualism and survival of the fittest are not a good basis for holding any group together, including the elite.

Lunatics running the free market asylum

If the current manifestation of the Establishment is no longer tied together by either shared class or collective interests, how does it maintain coherence? For Owen Jones, Anthony Sampson and other recent Establishment accounts, the answer is to be located in the ideas of neoliberalism: that is, everything to do with promoting the small state, the free market system, low taxes and low regulation, globalisation and so on. Disparate modern elites now share an ideology that both justifies and maintains their wealth and positions of power.

But does such a world-view provide a stable basis for the maintenance of elite power and profit? Almost four decades of neoliberal dominance over the political and economic system suggests that it does. It implies that, despite periodic shocks to the system, the Establishment will endure.

Arguably, this may no longer be the case. And all the clues are to be found in the City of London, now at the heart of British Establishment power. It is in the capital's financial sector where neoliberalism and self-interest have been dominant driving principles for far longer than anywhere else in UK. It is here where the Establishment almost wiped itself out and where they are most likely to finish the job in future.

Anyone who actually spends time researching the City can see the potential for things to collapse at short notice. The City is a strange mix of old oak Establishment and shiny new steel and glass anarchy. Underneath the calm veneers of its well-mannered, immaculately dressed inmates, no-one seems to trust anything or anyone else. Authors like Philip Augar[12] have documented how the death of 'gentlemanly capitalism' followed 'Big Bang' in 1985–86. More recently, Joris Luyendijk, in his *Swimming with Sharks*,[13] has shown how destructive an extended period of venal self-interest has proved to be for those who work there.

I have witnessed something similar during various investigations of the City over two decades. The most unnerving of these was in 2004 when speaking to over 30 top fund managers and financiers about their operations and the large dot-com crash of 2000. What was so disturbing was realising that not much had changed since 2000 and that many could still see the potential for greater crashes ahead.

One of these was David Bailey, then a company chairman, who had been in the City for 35 years. In that time, he had been a successful stockbroker, helped to set up London's Options market, advised on the technologies introduced in Big Bang, and gone on to be a non-executive director in several big City firms. He was welcoming, friendly and blokey. He knew everyone and was happy to name drop and gossip. He didn't stop talking for two hours.

The discussion began with the decline of traditional stockbroking but, because of his experiences, soon spread to investment banking, the Bank of England, top quoted companies and their CEOs, big pension funds, regulators and Gordon Brown. The topics changed but similar themes emerged.

Prior to Big Bang, the City was run by networks of old boys' clubs, where trust and 'my word is my bond' made things work. Competition was limited, slow and parochial. Collective interests were clear. The 'big boys' set aside their differences and would chip in when a crisis threatened one of their local oligopolies. In the economic crises of the 1970s, the big institutions, facilitated by the Bank of England, had come together to save the larger banks and stabilise the London Stock Market. But this had all fallen apart since the 1980s. The 'old boys' networks' had been broken up. The banks were too big, too powerful and too foreign to play by the old rules:

> In the old days, every bank used to go and have tea with the Governor of the Bank of England, probably on a monthly or quarterly basis. Well, do you think the boss of UBS or Dresdner Bank actually comes across and has tea now with the Governor of the Bank of England now? Bollocks. The Bank no longer has control of the banking structures because it used to be done by a nudge and a wink in the way that Britain has historically run the Commonwealth ... But they don't

have the power anymore to say we collectively are going to save that business over there and it's the same way the London Stock Exchange.

Another theme was the ignorance of those now in charge. Everything had become more complex and fast-moving. The maths deployed was becoming more advanced but the base assumptions to make the models work were becoming more simplistic and uncertain. Governments and regulators could not keep up. Investment banks did not know what their employees were up to or how to manage the risks they were building up. Non-executive directors and fund managers knew nothing about the businesses they controlled:

the investment bankers don't know how to manage these people. And it's leached out into the wider society of all major companies ... Putting the non-executives in charge of the business is a bit like taking me to the Olympics and saying: 'Well it's a choice between David Bailey, who occasionally runs for the bus, and Darren Campbell who trains seven days a week, and we'll stick David Bailey in the 200 meters.' ... How can they set the strategy? Madness. Madness. The fund managers are in charge but none of them know how to run a business. What does Paul Myners, a bloke who has run Gartmore Investment Management, now Chairman of Marks and Spencers, know about retail?

But, most of all, Bailey was concerned with the fact that no-one now seemed either in control or to take responsibility for what was happening: 'Nobody is an owner. Everybody is a bloody employee. They've all got an incentive to pay each other more'. The system of checks and balances in the markets had gone. Everyone was 'effectively bribed for taking part' because there was no personal ownership, stake or responsibility.

What made this worse was that deregulation had left the City riven with conflicts of interest, enabling insiders to now play all sides. The individual rewards could be astronomical but the penalties for failure were relatively modest. And no-one ever got caught. He explained how such a state of affairs was threatening established institutions everywhere:

If I came to you with a great big fat wallet and said: 'There's a casino over there. Here's the entry ticket. Take this wallet. Go in and play any game you like. If you win you get to take home 20% of the profit. If you lose I will just have the wallet back.' Now that is [Nick] Leeson, that was Barings.

Ultimately, the City was now driven even more by emotions, greed and ruthless self-interest but without personal responsibility. That meant that the whole system was now under threat. He maintained a jolly, friendly manner but also spoke in apocalyptic terms. 'Terrifying', 'the end of capitalism' and 'hugely vulnerable' were the phrases he used. The City was now peopled by 'predators', 'bandits' and 'rabid dogs', who rewarded themselves with huge salaries, bonuses and options, regardless of success or failure:

> Controlled self-interest was perfectly reasonable as a methodology. And the control had been, by and large, self-regulatory. Regulation has worked. Why? Because they knew that if they didn't self-control somebody else would come along and kick them a lot harder ... Once you have lost self-regulation, which is what we now have in the City, to all intents and purposes, then everything goes by the board. You get the lunatics running the asylum quite frankly ... Collectively, they behave like dogs that will pull down the structures around them and can, and will, rip them to pieces. It happens on a weekly basis that they will tear down a company or take over a company and then destroy it.

Remarkably, Bailey even predicted the likely causes of the financial crash and how it might play out, three years before it actually did: mad property prices and lending, derivatives, banks too big to fail and a Fed bailout. He was not the only one. Just a handful of economists and financiers are known to have gone public with dire warnings of what was to come.[14] There were a lot more insiders who suspected but who chose to keep quiet. A lot of these people, both insiders and outsiders, still see more of the same ahead. But venal self-interest means that most don't care.

Conclusion

The logics of neoliberalism and unbounded self-interest are as potentially destructive to the Establishment as they are to the rest of society. After decades, their flaws and contradictions are becoming too large to deal with.

They are also the cause of another contradictory flaw that threatens the Establishment. Both Robert Peston and Owen Jones recognised this one: that the new regime, for all its individualist and anti-state rhetoric, still depends on the state. Elites require a rule of law, security, a transport infrastructure, an able workforce and social stability to function. But neoliberalism promotes an ever-smaller state, a poorer, less able employee pool, and nods through corporate and super-rich tax evasion on an industrial scale.

The international transiency of the new elite means they care little about the spaces, communities or workforces that are essential for servicing big corporations, as well as their personal needs. All of which suggests that the current manifestation of the Establishment, if we can still call it that, has an extremely limited future.

As the next chapter makes clear, the new philosophy has now been disseminated across other parts of the Establishment too. Self-interest and competition has left politicians willing to destroy their parties, civil servants their departments, chief executives their companies, and journalists their publications. If that is the case, then who or what will remain to maintain the infrastructure that supports the Establishment itself?

Notes

1 Owen Jones (2014) *The Establishment and How They Get Away with it*, London: Allen Lane.
2 A.J.P. Taylor and Henry Fairlie are credited with first popularising the Establishment term. A.J.P. Taylor (1953) *New Statesman*, 8 August, Vol. 46, pp. 236–7; Henry Fairlie (1955) *The Spectator*, 23 September, pp. 379–80.
3 Hugh Thomas ed. (1959) *The Establishment*, London: Anthony Blond Ltd; Anthony Sampson (1962) *Anatomy of Britain*, London: Hodder and Stoughton.
4 The Clarendon schools are named after the Clarendon Commission of 1861. This investigated Britain's leading private boarding schools, focusing on: Eton, Harrow, Rugby, Charterhouse, Shrewsbury, Westminster and Winchester.
5 Jeremy Paxman (1990) *Friends in High Places: Who Runs Britain*? London: Penguin; Andrew Adonis and Stephen Pollard (1997) *A Class Act: The Myth of Britain's Classless Society*, London: Penguin.
6 Anthony Sampson (2004) *Who Runs this Place? The Anatomy of Britain in the 21st Century*, London: John Murray.

7 Philip Stanworth and Anthony Giddens eds. (1974) *Elites and Power in British Society*, Cambridge: Cambridge University Press.

8 Peter Barberis (1996) *The Elite of the Elite: Permanent Secretaries in the British Higher Civil Service*, Brookfield, Vt: Dartmouth Pub. Co.

9 Commission for Social Mobility (2014) *Elitist Britain*, London: Commission for Social Mobility.

10 Robert Peston (2008) *Who Runs Britain ... And Who's to Blame for the Economic Mess We're in?* London: Hodder.

11 George Orwell (2017 [1941]) *England Your England*, London: Penguin, pp. 29–30.

12 Philip Augar (2000) *The Death of Gentlemanly Capitalism*, London: Allen Lane.

13 Joris Luyendijk (2015) *Swimming with Sharks: My Journey into the World of the Bankers*, London: Guardian Books.

14 Economists like Steve Keen, Nouriel Roubini, Ann Pettifor, Raghuram Rajan.

2   Elites against the institution

Introduction

In the modern system of British elite rule, leaders have come to succeed almost by undermining the very institutions they manage. The ethos of venal self-interest has produced a series of individual risk-reward structures that conflict with organisational objectives. Thus modern British-based elites do well by transforming institutions into something they were never meant to be: short-termist[1] organisations for dealing with other elites rather than catering to publics and society. This shift not only erodes social cohesion, it destabilises the same institutional hierarchies and power structures that underpin elite rule itself.[2]

At various points, I've spent time exploring the national news media, the financial sector, big corporations, the Whitehall civil service and political parties at Westminster. In each case, I've found myself witnessing an institutional metamorphosis in the organisations at their centre. They have stopped doing what they were originally developed to do and for whom they were doing it. Adapting to survive and compete has resulted in an entirely new raison d'être that, perversely, challenges their own original remit.

Those who work within them have adapted accordingly. Journalists no longer investigate stories and speak truth to power. They process 'churnalism' and speak the post-truths of elites. Politicians succeed by better managing big elite networks rather than by representing those who originally founded their parties. Financiers no longer allocate capital to the real economy but prefer to trade it amongst themselves. The new captains of industry make more profit by being less entrepreneurial, making fewer things and cutting employment. And civil servants working in government spend their time trying to dismantle their departments and outsource their own jobs.

And for today's leaders, personal success means achieving these organisational aims and objectives more efficiently and ruthlessly than their predecessors. The results are fewer news consumers, party members, companies, employees and engaged citizens. Eventually, that erosion of the public base also means the destabilisation of those same institutions through which elite power is wielded.

Journalism turns into churnalism

Britain has long proclaimed pride in its independent, objective, high-quality news sector – its BBC, its international news service and its long-established press. Presented as an enquiring 'fourth estate' that holds the powerful to account, it is a foundation stone of British democracy. Or so those media mogul owners and members of the Establishment keep proclaiming. The public is no longer convinced. They have stopped trusting its output and are rather less willing to pay for it.

This decline isn't simply because Britain's media has a long tradition of supporting the Conservative Party and the Establishment.[3] A key problem is also that the industry has almost imperceptibly morphed into a mass generator of material that barely qualifies as news. The notion that Britain still has a respected, autonomous news media is, itself, a post-truth construction. How did this happen and when did it begin?

The decline has been a slow but steady trend, taking place over several decades. Readers and advertising have been trickling away. The response of media owners has been to cut costs while demanding the same rates of return. Doing this, year after year, has had a similar effect to imposing austerity on public services. The output has become a shadow of what it was, turning journalism into what Nick Davies has called 'Churnalism'.[4]

One clear indicator of this can be found in the expanding public relations industry and its growing influence over news content. The links between PR and news are most often made in relation to the New Labour era. In the 1990s, political commentators became concerned about the new breed of political news managers. But this obsession with spin doctors obscured the growing influence of PR across most news sections. Spin was already being widely taken up well before Alastair Campbell and Peter Mandelson began rebranding their party.

Its successful rise was not simply down to some intimidating, former hacks making life unbearable for brave, truth-seeking journos. The reality was more mundane. Simply put, PR was becoming a very useful means for journalists needing to cut corners in a hurry. It had become a secret information subsidy that correspondents knew all about but were loath to speak of in public.[5] As Jon Snow of *Channel Four News* typically explained: 'you can't differentiate between a spin doctor and a source. Many of the recipients of spin doctors are very happy to hear from them ... It isn't simply nasty spin doctor hassling innocent victim journalist.'

What was an occasional, quick-fix drug in the 1980s became a regular addiction in the 1990s. Michael Walters was one of those who drew on his 21 years in business news to explain what had been happening. When we met in the late 1990s, he had just left his position as Deputy City Editor of the *Daily Mail*. It was his first week being employed in financial public relations. He was relieved to have switched into PR but also bitter about the circumstances that had forced him to leave journalism. When he began, it was a much better resourced sector. He took pride in the expertise he built up and the effort he put into gaining his own source material. He tried to offer genuine, independent analysis for his small investor readers. But then it all began to change. Income dropped but management tried to maintain the same healthy profits:

> I got totally pissed off at the starving of resources at the *Mail* ... Perversely, as the new technology has come in, copy times have got shorter. As the print run gets longer your day gets shorter. The *Mail* is one particular case, and we didn't keep up. I've left, quite frankly, because I am furious. The paper has been starved of editorial resources ... It's not so much the absolute numbers but the experience that's key. Many papers have traded down, bringing less experienced people into the paper. The papers themselves are going increasingly down market.

The story was a common one. Editorial and investigative resources were being cut but the demands for more copy per individual kept going up. Experienced journalists were being replaced with younger, cheaper ones. There was a constant temptation to cut corners and take the easy route to hitting the word count; the easy route being take the source material and don't ask questions, let alone go and find independent informants or investigate. As Walters continued:

> In a way, the vacuum is filled much more easily by PR. They offer you an interview or some other source – and you have to be very stubborn minded to pursue an investigative story on your own. The companies don't like it, the PRs don't like it, the brokers are against it and the City don't want a knocking story. There's a million and one reasons why you can't do it. But if you want to do a positive investigative piece then everyone will help you. Generally, I think it's absolutely appalling. It's not just PR led – it's editor led ... I'm just extremely angry about the whole thing. I expected to be in financial journalism for the rest of my life and, if I had the choice, I still would be.

At the time of this interview, the *Mail* was a relatively wealthy paper with a circulation second only to the *Sun*. Its financial pages also brought in lucrative advertising shots. If this was the state of financial news on a successful paper, what about others and where was this all going to lead?

Move forward a decade, towards the latter years of New Labour, and things were indeed getting worse. Competition was intensifying in the industry, with more players and 24-hour news. As Michael White, the *Guardian*'s veteran Political Editor, recalled: 'There are two fundamental changes since when I first came here ... the news media is highly competitive, it's much more marketised than it was, and there's a lot more of it'.

Restructuring was a regular occurrence in the face of declining revenues and sales. According to Nick Davies, journalists were now having to fill three times as much news space as they did in the mid-1980s. Journalists no longer had time to actually talk to sources or research what they were doing. As Barrie Clement at the *Independent* explained, 'with less reporters the papers think twice about sending people out to get stories. It's much more bums on seats now'. That meant that: 'Some people get 80% of their materials from the internet and wires.'

Worst of all for reporters, editors actively discouraged lengthy and costly investigative work. Personality stories and scandals sold more papers than uncovering more significant political problems.

As Trevor Kavanagh, Political Editor of the *Sun*, complained: 'The truth is that circulation actually goes down if there is a lot of political coverage – unless it's to do with a scandal.' For Colin Brown, of the *Independent*: 'We don't do serious investigations. If you've got a long-term investigation into, say, the Trident weapon programme, or you've got a minister getting his leg over with his secretary, you'll make a lot of money out of the second and you'll hardly get anybody to publish the first.'

These interviews took place shortly before the financial crash came, bringing a sudden drop in advertising spend. It was also before news audiences and advertising began migrating in large numbers to the online world. A few years later, the hacking scandal and Leveson Inquiry that followed gave a similar insight into what had been happening in national journalism. Industrial-scale hacking was really just another corner-cutting exercise – a way of generating a steady flow of celebrity stories on the cheap.

Today, British news reporting is viewed with deep distrust and cynicism. For some years it has come bottom of European surveys that ask about trust in news. In the 2005–9 World Values Survey, the UK had the second lowest trust rating of the 56 countries surveyed (the lowest was Australia, where Rupert Murdoch has reigned supreme for decades).[6] In 2017, it ranked 40th in the world on its press freedom score.[7] Even tiny, poor countries, with barely two newspapers to rub together, like Namibia and American Samoa, get higher scores than the UK.

Perhaps more significantly for its media mogul owners and the Establishment, the business model of news journalism is now well and truly broken. Sales of most national newspapers are somewhere between a quarter and a half of what they were when I first spoke to Michael Walters in the 1990s.[8] News operations have lost billions in advertising but have only gained millions for their online versions. Google and Facebook have over 80% of that market. They, and other news aggregators and bloggers, use traditional news content but they do little to pay for it. National news operations sound ever more hysterical as they attempt to compete with their clickbait alternatives by offering lurid, nonsensical and hate-filled front pages.

Despite all this, news owners and producers still portray themselves as investigators, truth-seekers, conveyors of public opinion and challengers of the elite. Indeed, they have resisted all public discussion of their financial plight or attempts at reform of their industry. They scream 'freedom of the press' and proclaim their vital role to democracy. But this projected image is the same kind of post-truth account that journalists themselves denounce. Much of the press, on the whole, is no more impartial and objective than its far-right billionaire owners will allow it to be.

Look behind the new page layouts and TV graphics and there is little left. They have run out of corners to cut. It's barely reworked public relations material and native advertising.[9] It's opinion and features, gimmicks and diary events. It's cut-and-pasted news wire fodder and plagiarised bits from other news operations. It's no more real than cheap, watered-down pub coke or a fake Rolex watch. It looks like news but it isn't. And the public knows it even if the Establishment doesn't.

Parties dump publics

The EU referendum campaign of 2016 revealed just how willing politicians had become to sacrifice everything to achieve their personal ambitions. The campaigns were not about left and right, or even remain against leave, but about winning control of the Conservative Party itself. News content was dominated by senior Conservative Party figures, big business leaders and, most of all, the Tory press. All others looked helplessly on as Michael Gove and Boris Johnson took on David Cameron and George Osborne. Nothing else mattered more than gaining power over the party – not the voters, not Britain, and not even the party itself.

This win-at-all-costs approach was nothing new for the Conservative Party (even if the willingness to sacrifice so much was). In many ways, this direction of travel was set for the Conservatives back in 2005. This was when David Cameron, who was to become both party saviour and destroyer, became leader.

In 2005, the Conservatives had just lost their third election and seemed no closer to finding a post-Thatcher identity. With her rejection of 'society' and cosy Establishment clubs, and her embrace of global markets, Mrs Thatcher had rejected the old Tory paternalism and one-nation philosophy. The 'nasty party' was now confused about its ideological direction. Blair's New Labour did capitalism with a kinder and more media-savvy face. As Ann Widdecombe later put it: 'What they actually want is the Tory agenda but they don't want the Tories.' A succession of traditional party leaders – William Hague, Iain Duncan-Smith, Michael Howard – came and went without finding a new way forward. And then, out of the Tory blue, came David Cameron.

Barely anyone outside Westminster had heard of him when he joined the leadership battle in 2005. However, he overtook several well-known Conservative front-bencher figures to win. A few years later I got to speak to some 40 MPs and journalists who had seen events from close up. Their accounts not only explained Cameron's success but, with hindsight, also gave some pointers towards what would eventually tear the party apart.

Simon Heffer, Associate Editor and lead commentator of the *Daily Telegraph*, appeared very much a traditional, Establishment Tory. If you fired an arrow into a large target that represented Conservative members, and you hit the very centre of that target, Heffer's marker would be there. He was, and is, pro-Section 28, pro-Christianity's influence on public policy, pro-tie-wearing, and pro-hereditary peers. He was also anti-'liberal society', anti-Europe and anti-globalisation. He was deeply antagonistic towards modern politicians who he thought seemed to know and believe in little, and to work for the kind of pay that would only attract the 'second rate'. In his view, Cameron, the party's dynamic young new leader, was no different:

> I'm rather affected by the fact that many politicians don't seem to have their own views ... I look at a lot of people in the Labour Party now who are clearly following a course that they don't believe. These are former Marxists and communists, which Blair wasn't of course, who are doing something for reasons of ambition. And that's also something that strikes me very much about the present leader of the Conservative Party; that he is somebody who is motivated by desire to be Prime Minister and not by a desire to fulfil a programme of political conviction.

Heffer wasn't alone in wondering if David Cameron and others still believed in anything. Until the recent rise of Jeremy Corbyn, journalists and politicians regularly grumbled about the end of ideology. Austin Mitchell barked over his tea in Portcullis House: 'This isn't an ideological electorate. It wouldn't recognise an ideology if it drove over them in a tank.' Several wondered aloud what Cameron actually stood for, beyond classic Thatcherism delivered in New

Labour-type packaging. Although Cameron had served a lengthy apprenticeship working as a researcher and advisor for several party leaders, his campaign offered few hard policies.

His primary aims were to detoxify the party's image and to be seen as 'the heir to Blair'. He succeeded, later going on to hug huskies and spout 'compassionate conservativism'. At the time, Cameron didn't just adopt New Labour's third-way policy pragmatism, he closely studied Blair's biographies as a military historian might consume Sun Tzu's *The Art of War*. It was all about media management, public performance, seizing the centre ground and spin.

Cameron's more established leadership opponents, such as David Davis and Ken Clarke, set out their policy stalls and canvassed their parliamentary colleagues. Cameron instead pulled together a core group of seasoned journalists and public relations specialists. Ironically, from a post-2016 perspective, his core group included Steve Hilton of Saatchi and Saatchi, and the former hacks Boris Johnson and Michael Gove.

For Chris Grayling and Iain Dale, heading David Davis's campaign, it was clear that team Cameron was prepared to do a lot of things they found rather distasteful. They focused intently on lobbying key media figures in the long run-up to the official campaign. They managed to get journalists to write Cameron up as the 'new Blair', with George Osborne the 'new Brown'. Some 70 articles in this period make this association. They circulated DVDs of focus groups enthusing about him to all Conservative MPs and political commentators. They carefully managed all public events. They knew every trick in the spin handbook. Dale recounted how this played out during the party conference speeches, when David Davis appeared to falter:

> Tom Bradby did a report for ITN, which said 'the speech totally bombed'. He showed people asleep in the audience ... Now, that was helped by some good briefing by the Cameron people, who had sort of made sure that a lot of their supporters were sat in front of the press desks, and didn't give David Davis a standing ovation. I mean, in a sense I rather admire him for that, in a perverse sort of way.

For Tom Bradby and several other journalists who were there at the time, it was less about them and more about what they picked up from the aging party faithful in the audience. The word used several times was 'winner'. The party had lost three elections and had five more years of opposition to go. They wanted someone who looked like they could win and they stopped caring that much about what Cameron stood for. Interestingly enough, the best summing up of events came from the Labour minister David Blunkett:

> I thought that the collective instinctive decision of the media gathered in Blackpool that David Davis had failed and that David Cameron was the born-again Blair was absolutely profound in terms of the impact it had, not merely in terms of the Conservative Party, but the perceptions outside … And, therefore, the new benchmark was different to the old one. Instead of it being experience, knowledge, hands-on in Parliament, dealing with big issues, gravitas, that benchmark was then subsumed entirely. And the new benchmark of the presentable, the fresh, the new, the ability to ditch policy, and image, that became then the judgement that had to be made.

What was equally interesting about Blunkett's analysis was that it referred just as much to his own party. Blair and Cameron did have a lot in common. Both refashioned their parties to become election winners. Both were more interested in party management and playing the statesman than policy development. Both tried to secure the fabled 'centre ground'. Both came to spend more time with big funders, media moguls, campaign experts and the more exclusive parts of the Westminster Village then they did their MPs or ordinary supporters. And, in making themselves and their parties 'winners', they jettisoned traditional members, voters and core ideologies. Such developments have been well documented in Colin Crouch's *Post-Democracy* and Peter Mair's *Ruling the Void*.[10]

The consequences of both parties reinventing themselves as election winners, rather than representative parties, have been predictable. Since the 1950s, election turnout has dropped an average of 20%, reaching a low point of 60% in 2001. In 1983 party membership amounted to 3.8% of the population but by 2013 it was 0.8%.[11] The figures for 'trust' in politicians and established 'party identification' have also continued to decline steadily. Long-established loyalties to parties have been broken as electoral volatility has grown enormously.

2016 was the year that ordinary people hit back, with many voting as much for the anti-Establishment candidates as along traditional party lines. The political elite in Britain, as in the US, France, Greece and Spain, were being given a good kicking. They got the Doc Martins out again in June 2017 as they ignored the political and media establishment at Westminster (both Conservative and Blairite). As Christopher Hitchens commented in the *Mail on Sunday*, May's Conservative Party failed 'because they have long believed in nothing and are interested only in being in office … just a cold machine which runs on gallons of expensive snake oil'.[12]

Civil servants outsource democracy

Today's top civil servants are caught between two conflicting professional visions. The older one relates to their role as public servants. They make the central machinery of government work, as well as delivering services, from health to policing, across the nation. They are, in their own words, 'objective', 'impartial' and 'accountable to the public'.[13] The more recent second vision is driven by neoliberalism. This assumes that government bureaucracies don't work well and should be shrunk whenever possible, with key functions run by the private sector.

Slowly the latter philosophy has become the dominant one, with critical consequences for both the civil service and public. As neoliberalism became more dominant, so successive governments came up with various formulas to shrink the state while also trying to maintain efficiency and public accountability. This began in the Thatcher years, when government-owned companies, land and assets were privatised and sold off.[14]

After that, the audit and new public management cultures of the private sector were imported and used to reconfigure the nation's bureaucracy.[15] New state institutions were built on the never never (also known as PPP or PFI). Traditional functions were outsourced to quangos and opaque multinationals.[16] With each of these steps, so objectivity, impartiality, public accountability and service have been eroded further.

There is no greater an example of this than the story of the DTI (Department of Trade and Industry) and British industrial policy. In the 1970s its two parts made up a large, influential entity in Whitehall. By the end of Mrs Thatcher's tenure, it had become a shadowy pariah that no ambitious civil servant or minister wanted to be associated with. It was temporarily resuscitated by New Labour before being scrapped altogether. Throughout, the department not only collaborated in its own demise, it made the whole concept of a national industrial policy appear obsolete. And in the process, it played a key part in the sell-out of British industry.

This became clear when talking to former ministers and civil servants who had served in the DTI and Treasury. One of those I interviewed started in the 1970s, and eventually got all the way to the top of the civil service. Now retired, she looks back over her time with a sense of critical distance, judging her younger self as she goes. Her story is of a 'wide-eyed Northern girl' who had not been in the service long when the new Thatcher government arrived: 'I was in Keith Joseph's office '81, '82. That was an absolutely seminal time in that everything around industrial policy, or the work of the DTI, was being rethought from absolutely first principle.'

Like others in Whitehall, she had been frustrated at government failures to manage the economy. She was inspired by Keith Joseph, Milton Friedman and the new Conservative think tanks. They were all forcing the debate into previously unthinkable territory: Britain needed a smaller state and stronger markets to compete in the global economy.

As she explained it, the pathway for ambitious and able juniors like herself lay in embracing the new philosophy. That meant selling off the national industries and stimulating competition everywhere. In effect, it meant she would succeed by shrinking her own department. She maintained her fast-stream advance by first working on privatisations, and then on competition and international trade policy:

> there was a constant drumbeat about move back the role of the state and move the boundary between what is in the public sector and what is in the private sector ... the direction was set in those very early years by Sir Keith and Mrs Thatcher. It was pretty tough if you had a different view as an official. But if you were in one of those pockets where you were dealing with the big privatisations, it was an extremely exciting time with a very clear sense of direction of what needed to be done, and a lot of energy around those particular activities. So those people who were aligned with the Number 10 agenda knew exactly what they were doing, what the objectives were and what the timetable was.

Few secretaries of state stayed more than a year in the DTI. Most, Michael Heseltine apart, either trod water or collaborated in winding down the department. In the Thatcher years its budget was halved and its headcount steadily cut. The national infrastructure to support industry was wound down. The National Enterprise Board, National Economic Development Council and its regional offices were all axed.

Another former Permanent Secretary in the DTI took up the story of the New Labour years. The party of the working classes initially came in with different ideas. But then its desire to impress big business and the markets outweighed its desire to intervene in the economy. As an ambitious junior before 1997, he too succeeded by going to work outside the department on free trade policy in Europe's evolving single market. Under New Labour he took a series of permanent secretary positions before 'coming home' to head the department. He also watched despairingly as ministers came and went rapidly without any ideas or policies. His department was serially restructured and under constant threat. He saw the best course of action as keeping ahead of his critics by shrinking the department faster than they demanded:

> Then in 2006/7 we decided off our own initiative, partly to do with the relations of the Treasury, that we needed to make some more staff savings … it was 25% headcount cut in the business facing part of the Department and actually 50% of the small business service. Part of that was to say to the Treasury: 'I'm going to make cuts in this area and you just get off my back'. Because there was a caricature that they could run it themselves with a phonebook and 30 people … The result of the changes was to reduce the Department's budget from over £6 billion to a bit below £1.5 billion.

Ultimately, the DTI didn't just terminate itself, it made the notion of a national industrial policy anathema. It also meant that UK industry suffered a faster decline than all its economic rivals over the same period. In 1970, UK manufacturing accounted for 30% of GDP, 16.3% of total world exports, and had trade surpluses of 4–6% annually; 35% of UK employment was in this sector. By 2010, 13% of GDP and 10% of total employment was in manufacturing and the UK was running a trade deficit in manufacturing of 2–4%.[17]

At the time of the interviews, both former mandarins looked back wistfully and wondered if things went too far. They spoke with some respect for Michael Heseltine, whose push for a more interventionist industrial policy was marginalised in their times. Under the coalition government, Lord Heseltine's ideas were back in vogue. Vince Cable was trying once again to reinvent an industrial policy, and George Osborne was proclaiming a new march of the makers. When I talked to Heseltine, he had just written a well-publicised report on economic regeneration. He was scathing about the self-destruction enacted in the past to UK industry but hopeful about his report recommendations (but was about to be politically stitched up once again):

> by and large if you look at the people who own Britain's largest companies, they're not British, they're international investment operations ... The long-term interest of this country, the industrial base, the scientific elements, the research and development facilities, the supply chains, all these things have no consequence at all. Well that is unlike any other capitalist economy, unlike any other, starting with America. And we parade it as a virtue. I don't think it is a virtue but that's one of the things the government disagreed with in my report.

What happened at the DTI was not a one-off. The civil service is half the size it was when Mrs Thatcher came to power, despite a population increase of 18% over the same period. The departments of health,[18] education, transport, work and pensions, culture and media, and the home office have all worked hard to make themselves redundant. A third of government expenditure on public services is now spent through opaque private providers.[19] It's no longer clear if the new regime still offers much accountability or makes the machinery of government work for the benefit of the nation.

Business leaders choose personal returns over company profits

Captains of industry and finance have become very adept at explaining their value to the British economy. Heads of industry make the economy go round by creating new companies and innovative products. Top financiers make the industrial machine go round by efficiently allocating capital in the economy. They all create jobs and taxable income. Read through any glossy report from the CBI or LSE[20] and its pages repeat these mantras. They are the 'wealth creators' that governments are so desperate to attract and support.

Unfortunately for the British economy and its workforce, the reality is rather different. Financiers have become more focused on extracting profits from financial markets than investing them in new industries and companies. Chief executives are more highly rewarded for raising share prices, cutting jobs and exploiting monopolies, rather than innovating and making long-term investments. And the new emerging industries of the hi-tech and gig economies make a lot more money by employing less people and avoiding taxes.

I've seen this again and again when talking to those same leaders of industry and finance. The brochures and personal introductions often give the official line. Edward Bonham-Carter, heading up Jupiter Asset Management, was one of those to roll out the public refrain:

> the stock market, by and large, is efficient at allocating capital. That's what 'stock market' means – market for stock coming from capital. So, it allocates capital, takes it away from companies that aren't getting the right returns and allocates it to areas where, risk adjusted, they are making higher returns.

However, if the City once operated like this it doesn't anymore. When big financiers start talking investment strategies and practices, another account emerges. In practice, it's all about 'making your alpha' quicker and bigger than the next man. If that means screwing the company, or investing your money in paper crash helmets or radioactive lollipops because everyone else is, then so be it. Simon Howard of 3i explained his reality:

> to say 'This is a good company. It will outperform over five years. I am going to buy it and just forget about it', is unlikely to be a defensible approach these days. Because if the share underperforms sharply for the first 12 months of holding it, your client is going to be extremely unhappy … You have to be realistic. You might think a company is hopeless but if it's going to go up for six months you probably need to buy it.

This alpha chasing by professional fund managers means putting money into companies with fast-rising share prices, regardless of their potential or how many people they employ. And that means incentivising chief executives to do whatever it takes to increase their share prices. In turn, FTSE company CEOs and their annual reports prioritise 'shareholder value'.

CEOs talk 'shareholder value' like financiers talk 'alpha'. Their pay and bonuses are invariably linked to share price performance. And the winners in today's corporate world do whatever they need to do to make their companies look desirable to investors and so push the share price up: takeovers, sell-offs, mass lay-offs, and an exotic variety of creative corner-cutting strategies. They do it even though the evidence says these things are likely to make the company worse off in the long-term.

When we spoke, Warren East had recently stepped down as CEO of ARM, one of the UK's few international success stories in the hi-tech sector. The company designs the microchips found in most of the world's smart phones and computers. As he was between jobs at that point, he was able to speak rather more freely about his dealings with big investors (he is now CEO at Rolls Royce, and ARM has been flogged off to a Japanese software company). As CEO at ARM, he had been put under regular pressure from fund managers to reduce the research budget, change his business model, load up debt and fire people; in short, anything to make company profits look better, sooner:

> This is a fundamental flaw in the public company system. The fund manager is completely motivated by delivering the best possible return for this year. And if the companies which deliver that best possible return this year aren't around next year that doesn't matter because there'll be other companies the fund manager can invest in. And that's always their argument. But it is a flaw, because it means that there is pressure to do sort of short-term things like that, which from a business point of view are not sustainable.

At the same time, financiers themselves, in chasing their alpha, have been incentivised to work against the long-term interests of the markets they operate in. Finance theory states that if everyone takes a ruthless self-interest approach, markets will be stronger and will reach a point of stable equilibrium that benefits the whole. This sounds better than 'greed is good' but is much the same.

So, they have a rational justification for continually pushing the boundaries and creating all sorts of investment strategies and opaque trading instruments. These are all designed to enable them to get more alpha than the next man. But, in the process, they just keep building up bigger and bigger system risks, instabilities and bubbles.

A few seasoned, cynical insiders explained this. One of them was Paul Woolley, an economist who had worked at the IMF and in investment banking, but now ran his own fund management company. As he explained, markets were good, but unbridled self-interest was not good for markets. In reality, it made markets less not more stable. He talked about three investment strategies commonly applied at the time – index tracking, momentum investing and hedge funds:

> It pays everybody individually to index but, collectively, the market suffers because there is no efficient pricing. However efficient or inefficient the market is it's a zero-sum gain. Second thing is momentum. It pays everyone to use momentum but momentum causes bubbles and collapses and is damaging. The third thing is hedge funds. It pays everyone to use them but, collectively, it's extremely damaging. We get a bubble like that in 1999 or 2000 which is highly damaging. We had half a trillion of fruitless investment in telecoms infrastructure as a result of that bubble.

Close to retirement, Woolley now felt a strong urge to tell all: 'I actually think, my whole interest in my declining years is to write about the dysfunctionality of markets. I actually think the market is potentially dangerously dysfunctional'. Not long after we spoke he did just that, bank-rolling the new 'Paul Woolley Centre for the Study of Capital Market Dysfunctionality' at the London School of Economics. His sense of timing was perfect, as that was the year Northern Rock collapsed and the financial system began seizing up.

These stories and trends are not exclusive to the UK. However, they have gone further and happened faster in Britain than just about any other major economy, including the USA. It's easier to do takeovers here. More company shares are owned by foreign investors and for less time. And the financial sector has become steadily bigger relative to the wider economy than any other major nation.[21] Some 97% of 'money' in the UK economy currently is just circulating around the financial sector. It is neither paper money nor capital lent to real firms and individuals operating in the real economy.[22]

And, all the while, CEO and financier pay rises keep reaching ever-greater heights, and this is in spite of minimal increases in company productivity or profits.

Conclusion: destroying it all from the inside

In history, there is often a sense that new, better and more meritocratic elites and institutions rise up to challenge and then replace old ones. The bourgeoisie displaces the nobility. Industrialists replace land owners, and financiers usurp industrialists. New political parties take the place of old ones.

However, for the most part, the destroyers of British Establishment institutions that I have met have operated from the inside. Organisations have competed with other organisations and, inside those organisations, elites have competed with other elites. In each case, the system of sticks and carrots that has been used to guide ambitious individuals has also set them at odds with their wider institutional ethos. Personal success has not been aligned with either institutional success or with the best interests of the wider society they are meant to serve.

How and why this system has developed is explored in the next three Parts. These focus on getting to the top, staying on top, and then exiting safely.

Notes

1 There have been several studies of the problems of short-termism in business and politics. One covering both of these is George Cox (2013) *Over-coming Short-Termism within British Business*, London: Labour Party.

2 See the classic elite studies of C. Wright Mills (1956) *The Power Elite*, Oxford: Oxford University Press; Robert Michels (1967 [1911]) *Political Parties*, New York: Free Press.

3 See, for example, Tom Mills (2016) *The BBC: Myth of a Public Service*, London: Verso. See also election coverage studies by Loughborough University's CRCC: http://blog.lboro.ac.uk/crcc/general-election/.

4 See Nick Davies's (2008) account in Flat Earth News, London: Chatto and Windus. Prior to that, critics were already using terms like Newszak and Infotainment.

5 See Aeron Davis (2002) *Public Relations Democracy*, Manchester: Manchester University Press.

6 See World Values site at: www.worldvaluessurvey.org/WVSDocumentation WV5.jsp.

7 Reporters Without Borders publish this annually at: https://rsf.org/en/ranking.

8 In 1997, the *Sun* sold an average of 3.88 million daily copies. By 2017 it was 1.67 million. In that period, the *Telegraph* dropped from 1.13 million to 472,000, the *Guardian* from 428,000 to 157,000, and the *Mirror* from 2.44 million to 725,000.

9 Native advertising is advertising material packaged in the house style of a publication, sometimes blurring the lines between journalism and promotion.

10 Colin Crouch (2004) *Post-Democracy*, Cambridge: Polity; Peter Mair (2013) *Ruling the Void: The Hollowing of Western Democracy*, London: Verso.

11 See Richard Keen and Vyara Apostolova (2017) *Membership of UK Political Parties*, House of Commons Briefing Paper SN05125.

12 Christopher Hitchens (11 June 2017) 'Theresa's Tories … As Useful as a Zombie on a Broken Bike', *Mail on Sunday*.

13 To be seen on the government's own website: www.gov.uk/government/organisations/civil-service/about.

14 See James Meek (2014) *Private Island: Why Britain Now Belongs to Someone Else*, London: Verso.

15 See M. Power (1997) *The Audit Society: Rituals of Verification*, Oxford: Oxford University Press; C. Hood (1995) 'The "New Public Management" in the 1980s: Variations on a Theme' in *Accounting, Organizations and Society*, Vol. 20, No. 2/3, pp. 93–109.

16 See Andrew Bowman et al. (2015) *What a Waste: Outsourcing and How it all Goes Wrong*, Manchester: Manchester University Press.

17 See figures in Aeron Davis and Catherine Walsh (2016) 'The Role of the State in the Financialization of the UK Economy' in *Political Studies*, Vol. 64, No. 3, pp. 66–682.

18 For a telling account of what has happened at the Department of Health, see Stewart Player and Colin Leys (2011) *The Plot Against the NHS*, London: Merlin Press.

19 See Tom Gash et al. (2013) *Making Public Services Work*, London: Institute for Government.

20 CBI: Confederation of British Industry; LSE: London Stock Exchange.

21 See Andy Haldane (2010) *The Contribution of the Financial Sector: Miracle or Mirage?* Speech at the Future of Finance Conference, LSE.

22 See John Kay (2016) *Other People's Money: Masters of the Universe or Servants of the People?* London: Profile Books.

Part II

GETTING TO THE TOP

3 Selling leaders

Introduction

For many leaders today, professional life is all about being a star salesperson. A great salesperson can sweep a customer off their feet. They make good eye contact and entice them in with a verbal embrace. For a few minutes, they are as intimate as a close friend. And then they are gone. The customer leaves with the item but also a slight sense of loss. Then they get home and realise they have bought a pile of crap.

I've barely met a leader who didn't instinctively sell something to me – their product, their organisation and, above all else, themselves. Sometimes it was overt. Often it was a barely conscious act. Whatever they were peddling, they exuded a mix of intensity and charisma. But then, just as quickly, the meeting was finished and they were gone. I had that familiar feeling of loss.

The problem is that leaders leave all those around them with a sense of loss and disconnect. For their employees, advisors and colleagues, loyalty is demanded but not reciprocated. Loyalty becomes a risky and often pointless investment. For voters and consumers, they promise more than can be delivered. And, of course, the outcome is disappointment, cynicism, infidelity and a lack of trust.

Selling leaders up close and personal

Political biographies of Bill Clinton, George W. Bush and Tony Blair, amongst others, observe a sort of magic ability to make instant, close personal contacts.[1] Each was well-known for his ability to tirelessly work a room of strangers. Several at Westminster had seen how Blair could perform in a social setting. As Polly Toynbee, the *Guardian* journalist, explained, this ability continued long after Iraq had fatally damaged him:

> Blair has become such a liability and such a disaster that he can no longer carry a particular policy ... but he can still take, every month, a room full of very hostile journalists and leave them gasping at the end of it, unable to think of anything else to attack him with. And come away with his position improved at the end of each month. At the end of the press conferences, his reputation goes up a bit. He's got Clinton talent.

Blair was a master seller amongst sellers but was by no means alone. Whichever part of the British elite I'm investigating, two things seem the same. The first is how often a leader's life appears to consist of endless meetings, many of which are with complete strangers. The second is the almost uncanny ability of these leaders to know how to make a quick personal impact on all in front of them. Such an existence requires the kind of energy levels most ordinary people can't plug into.

A large component of leadership seems to revolve around meetings. My interviews were arranged with diary secretaries, usually sandwiched between other meetings, at an exact time but some months in advance. An assistant would bring us together. Another would be hovering, ready to either get me out, or to usher the leader on to somewhere else. The busiest people were frequently interrupted with texts, calls and desperate looking staff trying to catch an eye. Jobbing journalists appeared to be able to manage these regular interruptions without hesitation. It was like their hands and heads were controlled by two separate brains.

If journalists seemed the most frenetic, politicians looked the most meetinged out. At Westminster there were Chamber sittings, select committee meetings, standing committee meetings, all-party group meetings, meetings with colleagues, journalists, lobbyists, interest groups, constituents (and 'bloody academics').

Several barely knew the time of day or who it was they were plonked down in front of. No-one seemed quite as wretched as a Liberal Democrat front-bencher. Lib Dems had few resources and people but lots of front-bench roles to fill. Simon Hughes was almost physically dragged to his seat and then on to a next appointment by his aide. Nick Clegg appeared punch drunk, looking wildly around to see who wanted him where next.

Meetings dominate the working lives of financiers and business leaders too. Many professional investors insist on seeing the management of the companies they invest in a few times a year. Numbers of meetings, like the size of their funds, seemed to be equated with status: 'We have at least 500, quite possibly more. I'm at 500' said one. 'Something like, for the UK equity side of the business, 700 meetings, maybe more, per year', stated another. Company chief executives are no different. Paul Walsh, CEO of Diageo, sighed deeply and grinned at the same time, before responding: 'The CEO title is probably now as much chief engagement officer as it is chief executive officer, because there are so many groups that need to be paid attention to.'

But here's the thing. With all those endless rounds of meetings, with all that non-stop, frenetic glad-handing, most leaders I've met never stop selling. Tired, sad, desperate, disillusioned, imprisoned, they still keep it up. Consciously or not, they are always selling themselves.

A few appeared quite modest. Some were quietly menacing. But once they had all got going, that leadership selling thing began to shine through. They personally took my coat or poured me a drink. I got a firm handshake and a formal welcome. Then, within minutes, we were on first name terms. Good eye contact was secured. They interwove stories of stunning success with moments of self-deprecation.

I almost wanted to hug some of them as I left. Even Dennis Skinner, the 'Beast of Bolsover', who wondered if I was 'another fucking useless academic' before we began, got me grinning stupidly by the time I left his room. Even Ann 'Doris Karloff' Widdecombe and George 'freezer bags' Osborne were open and charming in the privacy of their offices.

It wasn't just politicians who sold a piece of themselves. Journalists impressed with who and what they knew. They could speak fluent headline and soundbite. Fund managers dazzled with science as they explained the superiority of their investment strategies. They all had the print-outs to show how they consistently outperformed the index, even though that was statistically impossible.

CEOs were on a par with government ministers. They preached business strategies and exuded calm control. They knew how to build teams and inspire those below. Intimidating figures, like Sir

Michael 'Mick the Miner' Davis, spoke with a charged presence. It was impossible not to like Sir Ian Cheshire of B&Q. Gareth Davis, who led Imperial Tobacco to great success, and probably millions of smokers towards lung cancer, was an incredibly warm, charming man.

Of course, none of the leaders I was awed by would be likely to remember my name two days later. But it was a surprisingly frank interview with Stephen Hester of RBS that really revealed all. Hester had just been put on 'gardening leave' by George Osborne and was in a slightly dour, reflective mood. He sounded quite alone sitting in his impressive Kensington home:

> I was shooting last week and there were eight people and I knew six of the eight and had known them for 30 years. Not that they were friends. Well, I mean, I'm friendly with them ... there are some successful businessmen for whom there's no dividing line. You know, their friends are their colleagues, their colleagues are their friends, and there's never a time when they're on duty or off duty. They're just the same all the time. It's probably a healthier way to be actually. For me, I had a very strong on/off switch.

You can know people in business for 30 years, see them frequently and partake in intense social exchanges. But they are not friends. And, since it's hard to tell a difference in the way many leaders behave with friends and non-friends alike, do they regard everyone as a friend or no-one?

This has a detrimental effect on people who work closely with those at the top. They see their leaders come and go, demanding much when present, but then quickly gone. Fidelity and application are demanded but not reciprocated. Continually watching your leaders move on must be difficult for those who have had intense, working relations with them and have had their loyalties tested under duress.

Such relations have also had a hardening effect on leaders themselves. Not only do elites live nomadic professional lives, they also change jobs with greater frequency than those below. Government ministers seldom last the full term of a Parliament. Nor do permanent secretaries in Whitehall. A third of FTSE 100 CEOs have been there less than two years, and another third less than five years.[2] For whatever reasons, ambitious top managers are forever moving on. The sociologist Richard Sennett has written about this phenomenon within large organisations in modern-day capitalism: 'The fragmentation of big institutions has left many people's lives in a fragmented state: the places they work more resembling train stations than villages ... Only a certain kind of human being can prosper in unstable, fragmentary social conditions.'[3]

That means leaders, in order to advance, must be prepared to ditch employees, organisations and even nations. And, clearly, in the higher circles of elite power, personal loyalties can be cast ruthlessly aside when needed. Prime ministers sacrifice ministers and advisors for their own personal, greater good. CEOs cull their top management teams and screw over lifelong business partners. Anyone can be expendable.

Sir Michael Davis was one who had experienced this – a double-cross of Hollywood B movie proportions. At the peak of his career, he was about to merge his Xstrata company with that of Glencore, led by his childhood friend Ivan Glasenberg. Together they were going to create the biggest mining company in the world. At the last moment, Glasenberg turned the merger into a hostile takeover, and Davis was left unemployed without warning.

Of course stories of double-cross at Westminster could be just as cut-throat, and losers were not offered golden parachutes. Former ministers struggled to hide their sense of betrayal after being dumped by party leaders, or out-manoeuvered by former allies. Treachery was also strongly felt when close confidants in the journalist lobby suddenly threw them to the blood-scenting press pack. David Blunkett only agreed to talk out of some cathartic need to 'set the record straight' on the unjust media brutality he had endured. Iain Duncan-Smith's jaw visibly clenched when the topic came up. Asked about his relationship with reporters, he responded with calm rage (never underestimate the anger of a 'quiet man'):

> The truth is journalists are out for one thing: a story. You know, they may be your friend, appear to be your friend today but tomorrow they may be cutting your throat because you happen to be the subject of a good story ... at the end of the day you don't really have a relationship with a journalist. This isn't really a relationship with obligations, it's a relationship with mutual usability.

Selling leadership through the media

Of course, selling oneself in person is not particularly efficient. Successful leaders also need to sell to the larger audiences that the mass media can generate. Accordingly, ambitious heads now have media spliced into their DNA.

In politics, elected MPs are virtually guaranteed to have had some form of media training. They might even have previously worked in media or public relations. They are almost certain to be a media junkie. MP's offices usually have some kind of news presence in the background – a 24-hour news channel or BBC Parliament tuned in, and news websites displayed on computers. It is also highly likely that they speak to several journalists each week and, if ministers, several per day. This mix of media experience, media obsession and personal journalist relations is very much the norm.[4]

The media obsession came across in many conversations. Austin Mitchell MP, a former journalist, mused, 'I think the media have in fact replaced Parliament. The real debate is now conducted in the media ... and we become participants in that debate.' And so, politicians have adapted themselves accordingly. The Conservative minister Ann Widdecombe explained that senior politicians were now so versed in journalese that 'you could write the headlines for them. You can have a real fun time writing the next day's headlines and you're nearly always right'.

For others, if you wanted to influence opposition ministers, or even your own party leaders, you did it most effectively by getting a critical news item rolling. Frank Field, former Labour minister, and now select committee champion, was as computer-literate as a pot plant. But he knew how to entice hacks to a good story that would upset someone in power (a skill he used to good effect when bringing down Philip Green). Politics by media worked, he concluded, because: 'the sad fact is if the Prime Minister reads it in the press he thinks it's real.'

The need to sell oneself through the Westminster mediasphere increases as one climbs the ladder because political leaders have become human brand logos for their parties. There is now considerable evidence to show that voters, starved of policy details and distrusting of spin and news, are more likely to vote based on their personal impressions of leaders.[5] More polls focus on the personal qualities of leaders than ever before. Accordingly, everyone connected to the Westminster bubble – politicians, advisors, journalists and commentators – see party heads as the greatest indicator of a party's fitness to govern. In every recent election, more media air time and copy is devoted to the main party leaders than to the rest of their parties. In the 2017 election, Theresa May and Jeremy Corbyn accounted for 56.8% of all coverage of individual politicians.[6]

Thus it is no coincidence that many recent party leaders and contenders have had previous professional experience in news media or public relations. David Cameron, Boris Johnson, Michael Gove, Ed Balls, Ed Miliband, Yvette Cooper, Nick Clegg and Chris Huhne have all had such stints before entering Parliament. Even Jeremy Corbyn has had some media as well as national campaign experience. Theresa May evidently has not.

For the same reason, an obsession with capturing media attention from the government drives everything in opposition. As the Conservative minister Damien Green, explained: 'the media is fairly predictable and is fairly susceptible to gimmicks, and therefore this is the temptation. And gimmicks that fit in with the general thrust of policy are a good idea.' Several hair-raising stories were told of how far politicians would go to sell themselves and their parties; how well-researched policies could be instantly dropped, or frivolous ones made up 'in the shower', all to catch a favourable news cycle.

One of the most comprehensive accounts came from the Conservative Chair of the Culture and Media Select Committee, John Whittingdale. He had witnessed the power the press could wield over media-fixated politicians (and was later to get his own personal dose over proposed new press regulations).[7] He had been part of every Tory administration from Mrs Thatcher onwards. He summarised each of the leaders, one by one. As he recalled, Mrs Thatcher:

> was somebody who did not care what the media said. John Major, on the other hand, cared deeply about what the media said and became obsessed with it. In opposition, the concern was just getting media coverage, and everything was judged on the basis of whether or not it would achieve that. William Hague ... he would say: 'we've got to have something which is newsworthy', and that meant a policy. And therefore, to some extent, policy was being created, in order to obtain the coverage for a speech ... during Iain Duncan-Smith's time, the same thing applied. The concern was always: 'how can we get coverage?' And the only way you get coverage was by saying something new, and by saying something new you were having to announce something. You are leaping on bandwagons because that's the way to get newspaper coverage.

It is not just politicians who are sold through the media. During the Thatcher years, while political hacks became focused on the likes of Tim Bell and Maurice Saatchi, media management techniques were being rolled out everywhere. Corporations of all kinds began employing whole battalions of PR people. There was a period of about five years in the early 1980s when the proportion of top companies using PR leapt from 25% to 85%.

Charities, NGOs and universities went this way too. Even the Royal Family and Church of England employed their own spin doctors. By the time New Labour entered office in 1997, Buckingham Palace had ten mini-Peter Mandelsons, and the BBC 34 aspiring Alastair Campbells to call their own (complicating any interpretation of *In the Thick of It*).[8] And all of these organisations had leaders to sell.

The biggest budgets and highest paid consultants are now to be found in large corporations. The top end of the profession is not in politics but in financial (investor) public relations. For this elite sector of the PR world, the daily targets are not Joe Public. Companies are far more interested in conquering the financial media and international investment community. And their most important sales asset is the company CEO.

This becomes clear when talking to the heads of corporate affairs in large companies. They and their investor relations teams are, above all, tasked with catching the attention of big investors, so encouraging demand for shares. If that isn't via direct contact, it is through the financial press and analyst communities. CEOs, as well as being despatched on sales missions to the City, are now also media trained and shunted towards financial journalists.

Tony Golding, a former economist, analyst and investment banker, had a wide-angle view of how London's financial sector operated. Upon retiring, he wrote a book on the inner workings of the City. Its subtitle was 'Inside the great expectations machine',[9] which sums things up perfectly. He spoke about the many irrational elements of decision-making that lay beneath the rational veneer of the City. One of these was the regular selling of CEO reputations through the media:

> when the *FT* and the *Sunday Times* do profiles of business leaders, they are popular. This is a classic way of improving the image of the company. This obsession with the chief executive as hero is very

dangerous. It even affects institutional investors who know it can't be true. One man or woman doesn't run the company alone. It is a star system ... The City, in particular, has a habit of looking at the whites of the eyes and saying 'Has he got a good pedigree? Do we trust him? Is he a guy with a reputation?' All those kinds of things. And you can only do that with a person. You can't do that with a company.

Financial journalists were even keener to talk to big-name CEOs. They tried to wine and dine a few a week. Just as celebrity stories helped flog tabloids, so captains of industry spiced up business news. And fund managers, underneath all the technical jargon and numbers, still put great weight on individual chief executives and their teams when deciding whether to buy or sell company shares. Industry surveys reveal that financiers are far more likely to refer to the 'quality of the management' than to the company's 'financial status' in their evaluations. Studies have also shown that share prices jump at the announcement that a 'celebrity CEO' has been appointed.[10]

Accordingly, many captains of industry are almost as media-oriented as politicians. Most are avid consumers of financial and business news. They reel off titles like the *Financial Times* and *Economist*, as well as business publications such as the *Harvard Business Review*. Equally importantly, unless they are part of private companies or primarily working with other businesses, they expect to deal with the media on a regular basis.

Stuart Rose, the former chief of Marks and Spencer, agreed to an interview at his West End club. He talked, without pause, in extended but entertaining monologues, while also discretely tapping away at his smart phone and smiling broadly at fellow members wondering by. As he explained, media appearances have been seamlessly integrated into his multi-tasking life:

> top managers need to be on the channel, they need to be able to handle the media. I mean, in my little way at Marks and Spencer, I used to get up in the morning or lie in bed for two minutes, and I'm thinking what am I doing today? Am I on TV, am I being photographed, am I giving a speech, aren't I giving a speech? Do I wear a tie, should I wear this? Which items of M and S am I going to wear? I've got to wear at least 50% M and S, so you just think about the whole thing. You are the personification of that brand ... the day you stop being a chief executive or a Prime Minister or a leader, then you can

go and behave privately. But when you're in, you're in public ownership.
So, I believe you've got to. It's part of the rules of the game.

From brief encounters to the end of the affair

All this hard-selling has drawbacks for both leaders and led. The first problem is that this skill-set is becoming all important in many leadership sectors, even though an ability to sell does not necessarily make one a good leader. Many people floating to the top – Blair, Cameron, Bush, Berlusconi, Schröder, Sarkozy and now Trump – are those who put selling first and everything else a distant second.

Clare Short, the former New Labour Cabinet member, spelled this out not long after leaving the Cabinet. In her assessment of Blair: 'He doesn't read detail and he's not very well-read. His superb skills are presentational, that's why he's there. But there's not a lot behind him.' In her view, New Labour had done away with its policy people, its experts, and with Cabinet debates altogether. Instead, Blair's style of 'sofa government' depended on an elite mix of shadowy technocrats and media Svengalis.[11] But, as she explained:

> It's not just about the character of Blair ... The circumstances throw up the people that can deal with the circumstances. This very voracious twenty-four hour media seems to be changing politics. Look at Bush, he's very similar to Blair. This sort of folksy Texan thing that works a charm in America, sort of good on the media, and a very tight entourage around him ... politicians who can handle the media come to the fore. So, you get Ronald Reagan, Arnold Schwarzenegger, Blair. It explains Bush. And, if so, are we in trouble. Because Churchill couldn't come through this. Attlee couldn't.

Second, over-selling leaders through media almost inevitably leads to disappointment. Ipsos-MORI has been asking people since 1983 which professions they have most trust in. This century, trust in politicians, which was already pretty low, has continued to sink. Trust in business leaders, bankers and journalists, particularly tabloid ones, is low too. It's difficult to guess who will win this race to the bottom, as leaders vie to join estate agents, double-glazing salespeople and other professional sellers down at the depths.

And, of course, it's the star salespeople who are likely to leave the most disappointed voters. During their tenures, George W. Bush and Tony Blair recorded both the highest and lowest post-war approval ratings for leaders in the US and UK respectively. In a six-week election period in 2017, an over-sold Theresa May dropped 44% in her personal approval ratings.

All too often, just like disappointed consumers with their new purchases, electorates have realised rather too late that they have been sold a pile of crap.

Notes

1 One of the best accounts of this personal, close-up charisma in the political world is Joe Klein's (1996) *Primary Colours*. Although fictional, it is all about Bill Clinton.

2 See Aeron Davis (2017) 'Sustaining Corporate Class Consciousness Across the New *Liquid Managerial Elite* in Britain' in *British Journal of Sociology*, Vol. 68, No. 2, pp. 234–53.

3 Richard Sennett (2006) *The Culture of the New Capitalism*, New Haven: Yale University Press, p. 2.

4 See Aeron Davis (2010) *Political Communication and Social Theory*, London: Routledge. Of the 60 interviewed in this study, just over four fifths had professional media experience and/or media training. On average, they consumed four to five different news sources, including three newspapers, each day. Two thirds spoke to journalists at least once a day and only two in total spoke to journalists less than once a week.

5 There are several studies that show large numbers of voters choosing the candidate on the basis of personal character traits and in spite of their policy preferences. For example, Lees' and Knuckey's chapters in D. Lilleker and J. Lees-Marshment eds. *Political Marketing: A Comparative Perspective*, Manchester: Manchester University Press; or K. Kenski, B. Hardy and K. Hall Jamieson (2010) *The Obama Victory: How Media, Money, and Message Shaped the 2008 Election*, Oxford: Oxford University Press.

6 See 2017 election coverage studies by Loughborough University's CRCC: http://blog.lboro.ac.uk/crcc/general-election/media-coverage-of-the-2017-general-election-campaign-report-4/.

7 As Culture Secretary, he was heavily implicated in scuppering attempts to create an independent regulator of the press. His activities appeared

fairly questionable as, at the time, the press had two revelatory stories about his sex life, with the hint of more to come.

8 For an account of the rise and spread of the UK public relations industry see Aeron Davis (2002) *Public Relations Democracy*, Manchester: Manchester University Press.

9 Tony Golding (2003) *The City: Inside the Great Expectations Machine*, 2nd edn, London: FT/Prentice Hall.

10 See R. Khurana (2002) *Searching for a Corporate Saviour: The Irrational Quest for Charismatic CEOs*, Princeton, NJ.: Princeton University Press.

11 See also Clare Short's inside account of Blair's operations in (2004) *An Honourable Deception?*, London: Free Press.

4   Rise of the greasy poll experts

Introduction

There's an old episode of *Yes Minister* where Jim Hacker is put in charge of making local government run more efficiently.[1] After a department meeting, one of the lower-ranking civil servants quietly comes up to him with a file of proposals. Hacker is impressed. He wonders why he hasn't met him before and asks why he is not more senior. The official responds with a resigned smile: 'Alas, I'm an expert.'

Today, it's pretty much impossible to be both an expert and a leader. In fact, trying to be an expert in anything when ascending the leadership mountain is a sure way to fail. It's like a long-distance runner trying to compete while carrying a bowling ball. Being in charge means making decisions about multiple things, and drawing on excessive amounts of specialist information to do so. And, no sooner has a leader mastered their domain then they are moving on.

But those at the top do have some things that they are expert in. These relate to getting to the top. Increasingly, those who get there have obtained the skill-sets and abilities to keep moving up. They are greasy poll experts rather than experts. Unfortunately, that also means that those who rise all the way may be ill-equipped to lead once there.

Greasy poll experts take charge

It's only when you speak to a leader with expertise that you realise how few of them there are. This became clear when talking to senior

Westminster figures at the end of the New Labour years. Older politicians and journalists would hark back to the Thatcher Cabinets. They were stuffed full of people who had had long careers in law, business and finance. They had lengthy political apprenticeships on the back benches before joining the senior ranks. They then applied that experience and acumen to their leadership roles.

This all seemed part of some quaint distant history in the Blair-Brown years, like a 1970s film, where everyone had big hair and flared trousers. Labour ministers typified the next political generation. They weren't from those old Establishment professions. They were younger and more dynamic. They did pop music and football. They surfed media waves and policy networks.

But not everyone at Labour's top table fitted in, and several of those had something in common. They were experts. Each of them had stuttered in their career, been quietly pushed out or resigned.

These were people like Frank Field, who became Minister for Welfare Reform, and had spent 11 years as a director of the Child Poverty Action Group and Low Pay Unit; Chris Smith, who headed up Culture, Media and Sport, had a PhD in English literature and many long-standing links to the arts; Estelle Morris, who eventually became Secretary of State for Education, and had 18 years teaching and working in education. Each of them had fallen foul of the Blair way of doing government. And it appeared that their expertise had something to do with it.

Nick Raynsford was another of those with expertise. Before becoming a Labour MP, he had been a local councillor, campaigner and consultant on housing issues for 20 years. This experience led him to a series of junior ministerial posts in housing, planning, construction and local government. But, despite his industriousness, he never quite made it to the top of government.

It became clear why when we met. Lacking in New Labour flair, he sounded a bit too considered and cerebral in his answers (like one of those advert boffins who do 'the science bit'). He made a point of sticking to areas within or close to his expertise, and carefully researched anything in his remit that he knew less about:

> I always feel more comfortable on territory that I fully understand. When I've had ministerial responsibility, I've wanted to get that same level of understanding ... I think where things can easily go wrong, is if ministers reach decisions without reference to sources of

information that they ought to be looking at. And then simply trying to make the policy fit the decision.

But he was clear that his approach was not that common. He was very critical of MPs who used their position to state a case they knew little about. They 'subcontracted their judgement to other people', and were too willing to be 'a mouthpiece' for an interest group they didn't really know. Too many were 'rent-a-mouths', just eager to get into the media whatever the topic. Moving on to the topic of ministerial rises and falls, it was clear that his unwillingness to adopt such practices had hindered his own rise:

> The danger is the trivialisation of politics. And it's associated with the kind of culture of spin and soundbite, where some politicians have felt it was enough, and indeed the only thing that they needed to do, was to learn the official line and then repeat it. Well I regard that as very unsatisfactory, and I think it increasingly shows where people haven't got a deep understanding of the subject but they're simply parroting pre-prepared lines to take. But that, of course, will earn them more brownie points than people who genuinely try to give a serious answer. Because usually serious answers have shades of grey within them, rather than absolute black and white. And party managers rather prefer black and white.

Looking across the main parties at the end of Gordon Brown's tenure it was clear that the political experts of yesteryear were becoming scarcer. A comparison of the 49 politicians making up the older and younger cohorts of the two front benches, revealed the trends.[2] The older lot had degrees, usually in law, history and politics. They had had lengthy pre-politics careers of 15 years on average, typically in business, finance, law, education and campaigning organisations. Most had also been local councillors. They took an average of nine years to reach cabinet level after entering Parliament.

The younger generation was very different. Half had a PPE degree from Oxford, purpose-made for aspiring politicians. Their pre-politics careers averaged seven to eight years but, in most cases, their pre-politics career was in politics. It involved working directly for a party-linked think tank or a political party, often as a ministerial advisor. It was also likely to include a stint in journalism or public relations. Few had been local councillors. They then took just over three years to reach cabinet level. Thus the newer generation of leaders had negligible careers outside of the Westminster Triangle and negligible experience of local politics.[3]

The younger generation of leaders did have expertise of a sort. But the expertise was that required to get to the top in politics: PPE, policy research, Westminster-style networking, journalism and public relations. In the 2015 general election, all three party leaders, as well as many in their top teams, fitted this profile. One of the most successful of this new generation explained to me just why this worked on a purely practical level:

> The reality is that politics has always been a career. And successful political leaders have often got into Parliament very early and applied themselves. And, I guess, at an early age as an adult, I got involved in politics professionally and was professional about it. I learnt my trade. So, by the time I was in my 30s or 40s I had 10 or 15 years on anyone who had been doing something else in the world.

Thus greasy poll expertise has become the most important form of expertise there is in politics. Michael Howard, the former Conservative Party leader, reflected on the new generation of top politicians: 'I think they all basically want to make the country a better place to live in. But there are some who are so entranced by the game of politics that it barely matters.' Jeremy Corbyn, more policy-oriented than most, and then a marginalised back-bencher, summed up matters well:

> I don't find in the current parliament, necessarily, lots of very well-informed people, penetratingly interested in lots of subjects. They're more interested in the political process than the causes, and I've been in parliament a long time … The ethos of Blair and New Labour is technical and media ability rather than knowledge of a subject. More so than any other leader there has ever been.

Something similar has happened in many leadership areas. Elites have little expert knowledge about the areas and organisations that they have to make actual decisions in. The skill-sets they have in greatest abundance are those most required to reach the top.

Fund managers invest billions in companies through stock markets in the UK and elsewhere. But, of the 22 I spoke to, hardly any had ever worked in the kind of company sector they put their money into.[4] It was also extremely rare for one of them to visit the operations of a company or to have contact with anyone other than the CEO and board directors.

Senior civil servants may have moved beyond Classics and become more professional, but that expertise is increasingly likely to be in economics and finance and in the practices of New Public Management.[5] They were financially literate technocrats first; with a knowledge of health, transport or welfare, second.

It was the same with the 30 business leaders interviewed. There were some with evident expertise in their industry. Peter Simpson of Anglian Water had two chemistry degrees and had taken a variety of operational roles while working his way up. Francis Salway, who ran the property development company Land Securities, had a degree in land economy. He had taken a sabbatical year in the middle of his career to research and write a book about the subject.

Ray O'Rourke of Laing O'Rourke didn't have a degree. But he did have 12 years hands-on experience before founding what was to eventually become one of the largest construction companies in the UK. He had done this bit by bit, always building on prior experience and knowledge: 'It's best that you operate inside a sector that you know something about. And being in construction and engineering is and was the starting point for me ... It's a progression.'

But such business leaders were now in the minority. Those who did engineering, a science or something creative like design, were declining in numbers. Instead, many had first degrees in business studies, management, accounting and economics. Back in the 1970s, only 7% of top CEOs had such a type of degree.[6] Now it was nearly half. Many also had MBAs. In 2014, 72% had one or more of these professional business-type qualifications. Several had worked for business consultants, like McKinsey's, or big accountancy firms, like PwC. They were professional managers rather than experts, creators or innovators.

Two areas of business expertise marked out many of these successful captains of industry. The first was their desire to reorganise companies. They did takeovers, mergers, disposals, restructures and down-sizing. Success was measured by change. Mark Wilson of Aviva used the word 'change' 44 times in our discussion: 'The other skill set that I'm very comfortable with is change ... Most people hate it. I love it. I'm very comfortable on change and pace and ambiguity, because then you can actually add value. If a business is really going well and flying, I would never take it on.'

The other area of expertise was in accounting and financial matters. Looking at the class of FTSE 100 CEOs in 2014, just over a quarter had a degree or professional qualification in accounting. Half had held a senior position in the financial wing of the company during their way up. In fact, this was the most common route to the top taken by a company head.

Like politicians, successful CEOs have moved away from traditional professions and areas of expertise. Like politicians, advancement is most likely achieved by having the kinds of expertise necessary to get to the top: business qualifications, accounting skills and an ability to push through change.

Power without knowledge

Whatever specialist knowledge leaders have when they get to the top it's almost impossible to maintain it once there. Expertise in any one subject area is quickly out of date. Decision-making extends into multiple jurisdictions. And each topic throws up a diverse array of information sources and an information overload problem. Each new advance in information technology only adds to the load. Any top person who says otherwise is either an idiot or a liar.

In the financial world, information appears to grow exponentially each decade. Each new stock exchange regulation, change in company law, or revision of corporate governance requires more. It is spewed out in great gushing geysers. And business journalists, analysts and financiers have to plunge in, desperate to fish out the useful bits. The fund manager Andy Brough cackled when asked about this: 'There's too much information. So, you could spend your life analysing things to the end and not coming to a decision. Like 100 years of solitude, that book by Gabriel Marquez. You get to the end, and there's nothing.'

Consequently, everyone who works in finance is always trying to find others who can help them find the useful bits. The financial relations man Paul Barber explained why his function is now so vital for business journalists: 'There are a large number of people with interests a mile wide and with knowledge an inch deep. Newspapers just don't have the specialists. Standards per se have not got worse. Your level of knowledge gets worse because there is just too much'.

Likewise, a financial analyst explained why his function is now so vital to fund managers: 'the broker's role is simply to break bulk, to be a specialist who is available to the fund manager to answer questions. The fund manager should not read all 150 pages of all the annual results statements. It would be a great waste of everybody's time if every fund manager had to read all 150 pages.'

Things are no different at Westminster. In any parliamentary year, there are thousands of bills, amendments and statutory instruments to debate, amend and vote on. There are also thousands of other committee meetings and breaking political news stories.[7] MPs also have to engage with constituents on multiple local matters at advice surgeries. Ministers or shadow ministers also have a detailed brief to keep on top of. To the casual observer it seems impossible to engage meaningfully with the large majority of political issues and legislation spinning through Parliament. Labour's Chris Bryant, a former vicar, explained his daily dilemma in New Testament terms:

> maybe there's 80 new laws a year and another 200 statutory instruments, and I would guess that out of those you can only ever possibly know really the ins and outs of ten in one year ... and you have no idea whether any of your source information is true or not. And that's quite complicated then. So, you do the kind of Matthew, Mark, Luke and John test which is if it's in several sources then it might be true. But, of course, Matthew, Mark and Luke are all based on Mark. So, it's not necessarily. And if Mark was wrong then it's all wrong, isn't it?

Politicians looked both harassed and embarrassed when asked questions about information in decision-making. Each day involved wading through mountains of letters, reports and emails on issues. They relied desperately on all manner of assistants, colleagues, briefings and the indefatigable parliamentary research services to help them bluff their way through. Rob Clements, head of these services, gave an insight into his day:

MPs, from all parties, phoning up and saying: 'Look, I'm on the radio in five minutes. Can you bring me up to date on this?' ... We try to meet deadlines, because Members forget that they've got a parliamentary question to the Prime Minister tomorrow, or they're appearing in committee the day after, or whatever it is ... And all the time, you know, the old joke: 'When do you want that?' 'I want it today', they laugh in a hollow way.

The people who know the least, but know it about the most number of topics, tend to be journalists. They are masters at sounding authoritative on subjects they didn't know existed five minutes ago. Sam Coates of *The Times* said in a hushed tone: 'You know, not every political journalist reads every report properly. They often just read the press release ... even well-known ones just don't get around to that.' Daisy McAndrew of *ITV News* laughed nervously as she revealed a little too much about the professional life of the TV news anchor:

> if you see a big story breaking on the telly, and you look, you can see the presenters Googling as they're broadcasting. Because they're thinking, you know, 'shit, Denis Healey, what did he do?' And that could be quite dangerous ... because you could get something wrong from Wikipedia.

Being a leader means inhabiting a world of one-page executive summaries and press releases. It means subcontracting out judgement to others who may, or may not, have a hidden agenda. It means behaving like an actor, confidently speaking lines that others have written for you. And, if you want to be an actual expert, and write your own lines, you are very likely to hit your glass ceiling.

Elite nomads and the loss of institutional memory

Those at the top of leadership hierarchies appear to move on ever quicker. This has consequences both for individuals and institutions. Elites have less time to understand their position, make decisions or develop a vision. Organisations lose institutional memory and cohesion.

In 2009, I was trying to find out more about WMD (weapons of mass destruction). More precisely, I was trying to tease out how the Blair government had obtained its evidence of WMD in Iraq.[8] After a lengthy delay, the Ministry of Defence put up a mid-ranking official called David Stevens, who turned out to be one of those experts buried deep in the civil service who rarely meet outsiders. At some point in the conversation it became clear he had been put forward for a reason. He was *the only* Iraq specialist left in the department who had been present during the 2003 War:

> One of the reasons why I'm, to a degree, probably valued around here, is the fact that I've been here eight years, which is very unusual. I don't think there's anyone on the Iraq side, and I do Iraq from reconnaissance. If you were on the policy side, there's no-one there doing Iraq who's been there more than two or three years. I'm the only person who is associated with Iraq who's been doing it constantly … it's just that the standard tour tends to be two to three years.

As he talked, he gave the impression of someone slowly losing the battle to keep things working as they should. Staff moved on regularly. The old classic manila departmental files had been done away with. The electronic equivalents were fragmented, had no chronology and gave no wider view. Policy information meetings were increasingly run by juniors, making it too easy for Number 10 to impose its preferred conclusions on the evidence. As he concluded: 'And, if anything has suffered, I suspect, in the electronic age, it's probably corporate memory.'

Several years later, this tendency to move on quickly had become widespread across the top tiers of Whitehall too. Of the 25 permanent-secretary posts listed, 11 had been in position less than two years. Only 4 had been there for more than four years. One of these was Nicholas Macpherson of the Treasury, who eventually lasted for 11 years. Baron Alistair Darling, when asked about senior civil servants, singled him out: 'this lot seem to have gone through an extraordinary number of permanent secretaries in the last four years. Nick Macpherson's the only one that's stayed there. He's now, by far, the Arsène Wenger of permanent secretaries, because the rest of them don't seem to last at all.'

If ministers had noticed the increasingly rapid turnover of top civil servants, so too, mandarins noticed something similar happening with ministers. As a Permanent Secretary of the now defunct DTI (Department of Trade and Industry), recalled:

> I had Alan Johnson for 6 months, Alistair Darling for 12, John Hutton for 15. And they're all talented politicians but the turnover was just ridiculous. In fact, when Alistair Darling left to go to the Treasury he said to me: 'You should be a Secretary of State for at least three years. One year to find out what the Department does and what you want to do with it, and the next 2 years to begin to do it.' And none of those three had had that opportunity.

The DTI apart, Alistair Darling did just about manage to stay for three years in his other four cabinet-level posts. But he turned out to be something of an Arsène Wenger himself. In the 13 years of New Labour, cabinet ministers had a rather faster turnover than premiership football managers. There were only two Chancellors of the Exchequer but eight Trade and Industry Secretaries, nine Transport Secretaries and ten heads of Work and Pensions.

Certain individuals rotated through cabinet posts on an almost annual basis. David Miliband had three posts in four years, Peter Hain five in six years, Alan Johnson five in five years, Ruth Kelly six in seven years, and John Reid seven in seven years. For the relatively small number of political commentators interested in real policy, the New Labour years were exasperating. Polly Toynbee, who took a keener interest in policy matters than most journalists, couldn't hide her frustration:

> People plucked in, plucked out, shuffled about. People who know quite a lot about what they're doing suddenly shuffled into things they know nothing about, for no very good reason … the numbers of DTI Ministers, the numbers of Europe Ministers for heaven's sake. Like chucking Margaret [Hodge] out of Children when she had created a policy, pushed it through, understood it totally, absolutely her field, but she had to learn it totally from scratch. There you are Margaret. Time to get dumped into DWP, where she has to learn incapacity benefits from scratch, mops up, shapes that policy, and then suddenly drop that, dumped into company law. I could go through whole successions of people … the civil service, same old mandarins playing the same old game. They just get randomly shuffled about in the same kind of

way by heads of department, they know nothing about. Knowledge, policy knowledge is undervalued.

Moving to the present and New Labour's time now looks like an era of relative tranquillity. Since 2015 there has been no continuity at all across the top ranks of any of the parties. Front bench posts at all three parties last for months not years. Labour and the Liberal Democrats have had had two leadership elections each. At the time of writing, the Tories are likely to have their second very soon. There are no Arsène Wengers at the top of politics anymore (or, by the time you read this, possibly not in football either).

If Alistair Darling was right about needing to be in post for at least three years to do anything meaningful, then the large majority of cabinet ministers of recent decades have been pretty ineffectual. Barely anyone in power since 2015 has stayed long enough to do anything at all. Enoch Powell's quote about all political lives ending in failure is no longer accurate, as that suggests a prior period of success. Rather, too many current political careers are better thought of as being composed of a series of seat-warming exercises that add up to a sludgy pool of mediocrity.

Conclusion

Today, in modern Britain, the main expertise required to be a leader is of the kind which helps you rise to the top. PPE degrees, networking and media skills for politicians; MBAs, disruptive change and accounting skills for chief executives; Economics degrees and New Public Management skills for mandarins. It's these skills and knowledge which enable budding leaders to get ahead of the pack. Any other forms of expert knowledge and experience is increasingly redundant. In fact, in many ways, it's worse than that; it's a drag on precious personal resources better expended elsewhere.

Those experts still in the system struggle to stay afloat. In the worlds of business and finance, creative entrepreneurs run up against financial short-term expediency. Innovators, who pay attention to research and development, move too slowly for the masters of the quick return. In the worlds of politics and government bureaucracy, the experts run up against political expediency. Knowledge depth is too slow for policy-by-soundbite politics. Attention to legislative detail has left them lumbering and flat-footed amid the turbo-charged networks of Westminster. In all these cases, leaders are failing almost as a consequence of their expertise, their attention to detail, and a desire to get it right.

Notes

1 Episode 2, Series 3 of *Yes Minister*. Broadcast on the BBC in November 1982.
2 See Aeron Davis (2010) *Political Communication and Social Theory*, London: Routledge.
3 See similar studies of MPs and political professionalisation, such as: P. Cairney (2007) 'The Professionalisation of MPs: Refining the "Politics-Facilitating" Explanation' in *Parliamentary Affairs*, Vol. 60, No. 2, pp. 212–33; P. Cowley (2012) 'Arise, Novice Leader! The Continuing Rise of the Career Politician in Britain' in *Politics*, Vol. 32, No. 1, pp. 31–8.
4 See Aeron Davis (2007) *The Mediation of Power*, London: Routledge.
5 See accounts in: C. Hood (1995) 'The "New Public Management" in the 1980s: Variations on a Theme' in *Accounting, Organizations and Society*, Vol. 20, No. 2/3, pp. 93–109; M. Moran (2003) *The British Regulatory State: High Modernism and Hyper-Innovation*, Oxford: Oxford University Press.
6 See studies in P. Stanworth and A. Giddens eds (1974) *Elites and Power in British Society*, Cambridge: Cambridge University Press; and also, M. Maclean, C. Harvey and J. Press (2006) *Business Elites and Corporate Governance in France and the UK*, Houndmills, Basingstoke: Palgrave Macmillan.
7 In 2015–16, there were 136 bills, 873 statutory instruments and 3586 amendments to consider. There were 416 general committee meetings and 1,104 select committee meetings. There were also 6,640 Library research briefings produced. See details in *House of Commons Commission 38th Annual Report*, London: House of Commons.
8 For the definitive account, see the long awaited Chilcot Report, published July 2016, London: House of Commons.

Part III

STAYING AT THE TOP

5 Different worlds, different cultures

Introduction

My own experience of investigating elite spaces reminds me of my global back-packing days years ago. Every place had its clothing styles, cultural codes, new phrases and jargon to learn. And no matter what attempts I made to blend in, it was always obvious to others that I was an outsider.

It's just the same with each new elite sector I research in the UK. Whether entering Parliament, the Square Mile[1] or a big corporate headquarters in the West End, there is a diverse and alien culture to experience. Such spaces are intense, insular and self-referencing. They evolve rapidly through a plethora of exchanges and communication. Agendas, fashions and terms come and go with great speed. Only seasoned inhabitants really know enough to take it in their stride.

Under such circumstances the everyday cultures of elites can become very different from those of ordinary people. Ideas, norms and values can be generated autonomously from within. The higher a leader goes the more removed they become. The constant danger is that those at the top come to believe that *their* world experience is *the* world's experience.

They then act on those misplaced views. Corrupt, self-serving practices become unquestioned. Leaders become obsessed with things no-one else cares about. They make decisions that affect those below in ways they can't possibly conceive.

Creating exclusive elite cultures

Entering an elite space usually means being confronted with both physical and social barriers. The physical ones, such as airport-style security systems, are easy enough to get through. The social ones pose a rather greater problem.

To become an employed professional, you need more than advanced qualifications. To be admitted, you also have to gain a certain amount of what the sociologist Pierre Bourdieu referred to as social and cultural capital.[2] You need to know some of the right people. You also need to have certain kinds of knowledge, to look right, to speak right and to be aware of the unspoken social codes in play. It is these things which mark the lines of distinction between those inside from everyone else outside. Elite spaces are just the same.

Parliament throws up an array of such social and cultural obstacles. One of these involves the unofficial entry requirements that operate in selecting candidates. Although diversity has improved, well-educated, middle-aged white males continue to take the majority of seats.[3] During the years of the 2010–15 coalition, 22% of MPs were women, 4% were in ethnic minorities, the average age was 50, 90% were graduates and a third were privately educated.

The everyday culture, languages and traditions are equally central to the separation process. The rules, customs and practices are a mixture of the written and unwritten, centuries old, recent or agreed for a temporary parliamentary period. Erskine May, the official 1000-plus page rule book for Parliament, is now in its 24th edition and costs over £400.[4] The main reason new politicians get away with screwing up is that everyone screws up a lot in their first years. As the Labour MP Sadiq Khan (now London Mayor) recounted: 'There is no proper induction, no little book about how to be an MP … a lot of it you learn on the job by watching other people, and by making your mistakes, and you hope that nobody's watching you when you make them.' Nick Clegg's account was more critical: 'it's sink or swim, it's the most brutal, medieval and, frankly, manageri-ally dysfunctional place you could possibly imagine. It's so full of unwritten rules and protocols, rituals and sort of ceremonial norms and standards that you just learn by basically making mistakes.'

It's also the intense, everyday levels of communication that generate the exclusive political culture of Parliament. That starts with those endless official meetings. When not in formal meetings, there are continual exchanges in the many bars and coffee shops dotted around the Estate. A substantial part of politics was, as Ben Brogan of the *Daily Mail* put it, local chit-chat and rumour: 'Ultimately, Westminster is a giant marketplace for political information and political gossip'.

There was always a need to know what others thought about any particular issue, who was up, who was down, who was on your side and who wasn't. The more MPs talked, the more they made it sound like a high-stakes version of *The Archers*. Michael Jack, the former Conservative government minister, reflected on his 23 years there:

One shouldn't under-estimate in politics good old-fashioned gossip. It's the bit that makes it interesting. It's the sort of chat-up in the tearoom. Talking to colleagues, people pick up all kinds of things. I mean we're professional acquirers and regurgitators of information. That's what we do ... It's no different than being in a sort of village. You talk to lots of other villagers. There are some villagers you're more sort of at home with than others, and you build up a view. Part of that is sort of an exchange of information but part is to find out what's going on behind the scenes ... there is so much speculation, and we all soak it up, because this is the next thrilling episode. The ultimate of the political soap opera is a leadership competition, because it changes every day. There's a new cast, there's something happening. It's all terribly exciting and interesting.

The longer politicians are there, and the higher they go, the more they get sucked into the culture and ideas of Westminster and Whitehall. Listening to Baroness Estelle Morris offered a particular insight into this process. Like most MPs who spoke to me, there had been a firm intention to 'keep in touch with the real world'. At each stage of her career, first as an MP, then junior minister, then Secretary of State, she still tried hard to keep up her constituency work: 'I did six advice bureaus a month, I had my constituency in the outer ring of Birmingham ... most days you're phoning the constituency office to keep up with casework.'

She then went on to describe how things changed the further up the ministerial ladder she went. Her time for constituents was squeezed. Her information sources narrowed. She moved out of Parliament. 'There is a tendency to do all the negotiating inwardly, so you do it with other staff and colleagues, with the Treasury, with Number 10'. Almost imperceptibly, she became separated from that 'real world':

The minute you get to be a minister physically, geographically your life revolves around the department. You've got an office there. That's where your meetings are. And ... it's quite weird. All of a sudden, the people you mix with everyday are not your own people, they're civil servants. You're surrounded by civil servants, and you're actually physically separated from members of your own party. I really felt that quite strongly when I became a minister.

Morris was one of the more down-to-earth politicians I met. Many of her answers on the more controversial policy decisions of her time sounded decidedly New Labourish though. She had begun working for the collective good and ended up hemmed in by collective cabinet responsibility.

This became a common story. Politicians were asked about their information sources, as well as how they gauged public opinion on issues. They employed a mixture of internal Westminster sources and external, public ones. For back-bench MPs, constituents were mentioned more frequently than anything else, and were given priority by most. But ministers, asked the same questions, had a very different answer: civil servants. Civil servants filtered and supplied all information on policy and consultations. They did the same with news media in the form of daily clippings. Whitehall-generated and sifted information was prioritised far and above all else.[5]

London's financial spaces are not quite as confined as Whitehall and Westminster but they are even more exclusive and exclusionary. Many firms have moved outside the Square Mile to Canary Wharf, or beyond to another node in the global financial network. But City elites still have their own cultures and sub-cultures. These don't even begin with a connection to 'the real world'.

At the top of business and finance, it is even more dominated by well-educated, white males from wealthier backgrounds. In 2016, only 14% of executive board members of financial institutions, and just seven FTSE 100 CEOs, were women.[6] The recruitment process also has clear biases which favour those from wealthier class backgrounds and education. Those displaying the wrong social and cultural capital, say brown shoes instead of black, are less likely to make the cut.[7]

The City of London Corporation has more authority and independence than any other local authority. It has its own police force, electoral and political system. I have visited over 80 offices in the Square Mile or Canary Wharf. Every one of them has a sophisticated security system. Dress codes are always clear: dark, classic and expensive. The language used is full of jargon and acronyms. There are no *Guardians*, *Independents* or tabloids anywhere to be seen. Lobby areas always have the *FT*, a range of business and international publications, and usually the *Telegraph* and *Times*.

There exists a long-hours work ethos and many exclusive social and practical facilities, enabling participants to extend their time there. The sector contains a number of overlapping elite communications networks with exchanges taking place on multiple, intense levels. The culture, practices, language and communications of these networks is as extensive as any other observed, self-contained culture.

Like Westminster, everyone is always talking to and observing what everyone else in their network is doing. As John Jay, then City Editor of the *Sunday Times* (now a fund manager) said: 'My diary is still full of lunches with chairmen and chief executives. That hasn't changed ... But in the end, it's a village. They need you as much as you need them.' Financiers want to know what's up, what's down, who's up and who's about to get canned. They want to work out what direction any company, financial instrument or market is going in. As Gordon Midgley of the Fund Managers Association, put it: 'This is a market where everyone sees everything all the time. Because everyone is competing all the time and selling all the time.'

Under these conditions, elite spaces and networks generate their own cultures, languages and norms. In the short-term, ideas and fashions arrive like plagues of locusts, consume all, and then disappear without trace. In the long-term, ideologies with a deep hold are consolidated and spread across a sector.

Media produced by elites for elites

The national news media is supposed to be the means by which these elite ideas and practices are challenged. Journalists are meant to hold those in power to account, by making leadership more transparent and contestable. The problem is that they don't most of the time. The larger truth is that news is often written by elites for elites. Outsiders, like a shadow puppet audience, are left trying to work out what exactly is going on.

This first became clear to me when talking to investor relations directors operating in the City. They had worked out long ago that it was pointless communicating with thousands of small investors.

As one said: 'The way the City operates it doesn't give a toss about the private investor'. As they all knew, it was the few big ones and their advisors who really counted. That usually amounted to 50 to 100 people.

It was Tim Jackaman, Chairman of Square Mile, who took the time to explain to me how it all worked. Jackaman was a rare humanities graduate operating successfully inside the City. He saw how things operated in anthropological and linguistic terms. Like others, he concluded that 'the private investor, most of the time, is regarded as an irrelevance. Ninety per cent of shares are now held by institutions'. This was a key consideration when providing information to analysts and financial journalists. At one point in the conversation, Jackaman got out that day's *Financial Times* and proceeded to give me a lesson in financial linguistics. With each article in the 'companies and markets' section, he began translating the true meanings of the figures and phrases being used. Although the *FT* had several hundred thousand readers, he figured only real City insiders would be able to decipher the subtexts encoded in these pieces:

> It's all in code and put out by the companies to prepare the market. Everyone in the City knows what it all means. It's prepared by City people for City people. It's all about conditioning the market and it's about careful management of people's expectations. It's all in neat columns and everyone knows where to look for them. In some cases, such as the *Sunday Telegraph*, the message is only aimed at about 25 people.

Speaking to business journalists corroborated what was happening. It's not that they were that aware of the codes in play in the barely altered press releases that were being reproduced in their 'news' sections. What was confirmed was how they too saw things through the eyes of the CEOs and big investors they talked to.[8] According to a senior *FT* reporter: 'For us it's the people who are running companies and investing in them that we write for. The company managers and the fund managers … There aren't any private investors.' Richard Northedge, Deputy Editor of *Sunday Business*, explained:

> On *Sunday Business*, we write for people who are in business. Certainly, we write for the captains of industry … The bread and butter stuff though is about business for business – take-overs, new directors and

other changes. People are interested in reading because they work in the company or have invested in it.

A very similar pattern can be observed back at Westminster. Political lobby journalists live and work not at their news outlets, but in offices at Parliament. Broadcasters have their studios just 100 meters away. Politicians may spend half their time in their constituencies outside of London, but reporters never venture beyond the M25.

Many seasoned hacks have been reporting there for rather longer than the average MP. They share the same social spaces as politicians. The political commentator Peter Oborne relayed his unease at the situation: 'Most of my colleagues are embedded journalists ... I think that the way in which lobby journalists become manifestations of the political system is quite disturbing.' Kevin Maguire of the *Mirror*, filled in the details about his time in the lobby during the New Labour years:

> I was aware of it when I first came into Parliament. I realised a lot of bollocks was written from the point of view of people in power. You get sucked into it because these are the people you mingle with and write for ... There's even a golfing mafia in Westminster. Journalists play with senior civil servants and advisors and other parliamentarians ... I was always marked out as a Brown man. Andrew Grice is seen as a Mandelson man. Others talk to Byers, some to Milburn, some to Prescott. Colin Brown, Prescott's biographer, speaks to him every weekend. Anthony Bevans of the *Express* talked to Mo Mowlam. Those relationships become part of the institution. You are a member of the club, which is what the House of Commons is.

In this environment, journalists are almost more part of the political culture at Westminster than politicians. They don't just report politics they *are* the politics.[9] They are message carriers for MPs trying to influence other MPs, on their own side as well as other parties. Clare Short reflected that 'Gordon never ever spoke in Cabinet to question anything, if there was an issue between Gordon and Tony, you know, you'd see it in the media'. Ann Widdecombe explained that 'most MPs, if not all, have one or two journalists whom they trust more than most, who they would talk to first if they wanted to get anything into the public domain'.

Just as with financial reporting, journalists come to interpret politics through politicians. Politicians are their main sources. They are the central characters in their stories. And they are key consumers and personal critics. George Jones of the *Daily Telegraph*, admitted that: 'Really you want to be in the position of setting the political agenda. And, in order to do that, you want to appeal to your fellow journalists and the political classes.' Andrew Grice, the *Independent*'s correspondent, explained his experience:

> it's easy to slip into a position where you are thinking more about the people you are mixing with, thinking about those in the Westminster Village. You are always aware of how articles might be perceived by your sources, be they back-benchers, ministers or spin doctors … People know every word I've written. They can remember every detail and every comma, sometimes from months ago. Often things I don't remember myself.

Ultimately, journalists and politicians get caught up in the same dynamic. Both sides claim to speak for the public on a range of political issues being thrashed out at Westminster. The irony is that, all too often, they are attempting to gauge what public opinion is by talking to each other.[10] The Labour MP Kevan Jones realised the scale of the problem as he struggled to reconcile his media-oriented Westminster world with that of his constituents:

> This place is a goldfish bowl which we move around in, and the press and the press lobby move around in. You can listen to Radio 4 in the morning and think that that's everything, you know. But when I go home at weekends and talk, people haven't got a clue what the *Today Programme* is, never even listen to it … if you say to people 'What's in the *Guardian*?', most of them haven't read the *Guardian* in their life … it's a very unique and strange environment, which means you are concentrating on the issues of the day. You know, the average person doesn't do that, do they? They don't wake up in the morning and think 'Oh, what am I going to think about the Education Bill today?', do they?

Elite cultures produce elite ideas

Elite cultures produce elitethink (groupthink on a larger scale), which can easily spread across an entire establishment network. Leaders follow blind fashions like lemmings over cliffs. Problematic practices become more widely adopted. Ideas, with little evidence, are uncritically accepted. Big ideas become bigger ideologies.

Under these circumstances, everyday routines can ease into corrupt practices. No-one questions them because everyone does them. The 2009 MPs expenses scandal implicated more politicians than not. The majority, those who were not prosecuted or forced to resign, were compelled to pay back part of their claims.[11] In 2011, the news hacking scandal broke, eventually revealing over 4000 documented cases of phone hacking. The Leveson Inquiry[12] that followed suggested the practice had become prevalent across Fleet Street, with editors appearing blind to its illegality.

Since the 2007–8 financial crash, widespread banking malpractices have been uncovered in Libor,[13] miss-sold payment protection insurance, money laundering and foreign exchange rigging. From 2010 to 2015, the total costs to UK banks, covering fines, compensation and legal fees, came to £54.6 billion.[14] In the wake of the Grenfell Tower disaster of 2017, it became clear that the flouting of fire regulations by developers and local council planning departments had become a common practice.

Beyond the normalisation of questionable practices, larger world views become entrenched within elite sectors. Such outlooks can be entirely out of kilter with those of the general public or economic reality. Across the City, there is a near universal belief in the notion that financial markets will always reach a natural equilibrium. This continues despite the fact that market bubbles are becoming ever larger and more frequent.

During the lead-up to the 2000 and 2007–8 financial crises, it was difficult for those in the sector to look beyond the prevailing wisdom. In the eight months before the crash in 2000, 90% of City fund managers believed the outlook for the UK economy over the next year would be positive.[15] The same sense of self-delusion was recorded in 2007.[16] For Roger Bootle, the veteran City economist, a lot of the crisis, pure and simple, could be put down to unchallenged financial market ideology:

> the *ideas* that underlay the disaster: the idea that markets know best; the idea that the markets are 'efficient'; the idea that there was no good reason to be concerned about the level and structure of pay in banking; the idea that bubbles cannot exist; the idea that in economic matters, human beings are always 'rational' … if you ever questioned,

never mind disputed, these ideas, you were regarded as a complete no-no.[17]

Among business leaders, there is a strong belief that free markets, deregulation and low taxes will benefit everyone. This translates into near universal support for the Conservative Party. Throughout the 1980s, polls of Captains of Industry found that only 1–2% voted Labour, while over 90% voted Conservative. Even in 1997, the year of Labour's landslide victory, only 7% voted Labour. In 2015, only 6% polled wanted a Labour government, while 87% wanted a Conservative or Conservative-led one.

Across Whitehall and Westminster, views on a range of political issues, from euthanasia to privatisation and constitutional affairs, can be starkly different from those of wider publics. The public have opposed every privatisation by a strong majority. MPs get very het up about constitutional affairs. But, for several decades, no more than 2% of the general public have regarded this as a voting issue.

It was such an elite bubble on EU membership which drove the 2016 referendum. For decades, MPs have had strong views, one way or another, about being in the European Union. Ministers and MPs, particularly Conservatives, were frustrated by the large swathes of EU laws and regulations being adopted, and the consequences for British sovereignty. Thus the UK's membership threatened to split the Conservative Party on several occasions (and still might).

But most of the time, the public have not been interested. EU affairs have been poorly reported for years. For the decade prior to the referendum, EU membership was barely ever considered a top-eight voting issue. It only registered as such as the referendum approached. Periodic surveys show that general knowledge about the functions of the EU is very poor. Just prior to the vote, a majority were unaware they even had MEP representatives. They had entirely misleading ideas about EU immigration and spending,[18] not helped by years of anti-EU reporting.

Ultimately, elements of Tory Establishment groupthink, blinded by myths rather than facts, drove the EU referendum. The obsessions of a small part of the Conservative Party and the Eurosceptic owners of the right-wing press drove the campaign. They had persuaded themselves that the UK, if liberated, would reproduce its past imperial economic ambitions. Britain would 'have its cake and eat it'. Unfortunately, for much of the population, it's not really working out that way.

Conclusion

Joining an elite of any kind means being immersed in the particular culture and ideas of that space. To stay in the club, it's easier to swim with that culture than against it. Going with the flow, whether that be adopting questionable practices, or moving with the bizarre fashions of the day, is far simpler. And, deferring to the general ideology is the norm. All this brings some form of stability amid the chaos of pressured, fast-moving spaces. But it can also build up problems that can have devastating outcomes.

What happens when leadership ideas are too divorced from either reality or large swathes of the public? How do elites manage and maintain control under these circumstances? One way is with secrets and lies, which takes us on to the next chapter.

Notes

1 The Square Mile is the nickname for London's financial district.
2 Pierre Bourdieu (1984) *Distinction: A Social Critique of the Judgement of Taste*, London: Routledge.
3 See Byron Criddle (2005) 'MPs and Candidates' in D. Kavanagh and D. Butler eds. *The British General Election of 2005*, Basingstoke: Palgrave Macmillan; or *Key Issue for the New Parliament 2010*, London: House of Commons.
4 See Malcom Jack et al., eds (2011) *Erskine May: Parliamentary Practice*, 24th edn, London: Butterworths Law.
5 See Aeron Davis (2015) 'Embedding and Disembedding of Political Elites: A Filter System Model' in *Sociological Review*, Vol. 63, No. 1, pp. 144–61.
6 See report by Yasmine Chinwala (2016) *Women in UK Financial Services in 2016*, London: New Financial.
7 See report by the Social Mobility Commission (2016) *Socio-Economic Diversity in Life Sciences and Investment Banking*, London: Social Mobility Commission.
8 For a fascinating account of how financial and economic news came to be captured by City and business elites, see Wayne Parsons (1989) *The Power of the Financial Press: Journalism and Economic Opinion in Britain and America*, London: Edward Elgar.
9 See study by Aeron Davis (2009) 'Journalist-Source Relations, Mediated Reflexivity and the Politics of Politics' in *Journalism Studies*, Vol. 10, No. 2, pp. 204–19.

10 This same point is well made in Susan Herbst's excellent study of US journalists and politicians, in (1998) *Reading Public Opinion: How Political Actors View the Democratic Process*, Chicago: Chicago University Press.

11 See list here: www.telegraph.co.uk/news/newstopics/mps-expenses/5297606/ MPs-expenses-Full-list-of-MPs-investigated-by-the-Telegraph.html.

12 See the Leveson Inquiry report (2012) at: http://webarchive.nationalarchives. gov.uk/20140122144906/www.levesoninquiry.org.uk/.

13 Libor is the acronym for London Interbank Offered Rate. It is the average interest rate banks charge to each other. This figure became subject to manipulation and fraud by insiders.

14 See CCP Research Foundation.

15 See chapter five of Aeron Davis (2007) *The Mediation of Power*, London: Routledge.

16 See account by Joris Luyendijk (2015) *Swimming with Sharks*, London: Guardian Books; or in the US by Michael Lewis (2011) *The Big Short*, London: Penguin.

17 Roger Bootle (2009) *The Trouble with Markets: Saving Capitalism From Itself*, London: Nicholas Brealey Publishing, pp. 21–2.

18 See Ipsos MORI (2016) *EU Referendum 2016*, London: Ipsos MORI.

6 Secrets and lies

Introduction

Lying is an occupational hazard for those at the top. It's hard to both sell and tell the complete truth. Keeping more of the people happy more of the time requires saying different things to different publics. And, naturally, those publics have cottoned on. A high degree of suspicion greets the words of campaigning politicians, super-rich bankers, tabloid media owners and over-paid CEOs. It's why such elites come so low down in surveys about trust and truthfulness.

Researching leaders, I've certainly encountered examples of what could only be described as bare-faced lying: politicians who supported the war in Iraq despite privately thinking there were no weapons of mass destruction; brokers and fund managers who kept selling dodgy financial securities when they could see a crash coming; civil servants who deliberately buried public interest reports; advisors who ignored the hard evidence that undermined the public policy; and journalists who pursued an eye-catching story that they knew to be misleading.

But what I've found more challenging is the lies that elites and institutions create for themselves. Leaders lie to themselves about the good they are doing. Institutions and professions present an entirely distorted public image of what they do. And larger-scale ideologies get perpetuated, in spite of their glaring contradictions. Leaders need lies, not just to persuade people, but because they need to persuade themselves.

Masters of self-deception

I'm not sure I've ever met a leader who is ruthlessly and entirely self-interested. Tough, back-stabbing and brutal? Maybe. Highly over-paid? Often. But, however they operated, they appeared to have mentally tied their actions to some positive, higher purpose. Those working for the state carry with them a notion of public service. Those in the private sector think they make a positive contribution to the economy and society. James Bond-style villainous megalomaniacs are few and far between (hard as that might be to believe in the age of Trump, Putin and EU referendums).

Interviewing 30 top CEOs was a confusing experience when it came to questions of business morality. A surprising number appeared to display a strong ethical outlook which conflicted with their business roles. A clear majority expressed strong neoliberal views[1] when it came to markets, deregulation and low taxes. They saw themselves as 'innovators' and 'wealth creators', generating employment and prosperity. They believed that they should be free to do this as they saw best.

Yet, a similar number sounded very concerned about social, ethical and environmental issues, of the kind that are associated with destructive business behaviours. Many sat on the boards of charities and arts foundations, or volunteered for government task forces. For most, there appeared to be no obvious links between what they practiced – capitalism – and certain unpleasant by-products of that – inequality,[2] exploitation, underfunded public services and environmental degradation.

Sir Terry Leahy was one of those I found puzzling. Leahy is regarded as one of Britain's stand-out business leaders of recent decades. As a board director and then CEO for 19 years, he relentlessly drove up Tesco's market share, eventually making it the UK's biggest retailer. Along the way, he picked up business leader awards like Meryl Streep does Oscar nominations.

Leahy's best-selling book, *Management in Ten Words*,[3] clearly links good management and strong morality. It has chapters with titles like Truth, Loyalty, Values and Trust. When we met, he referred to the robust family values he was brought up with and the principled code he follows: 'ultimately, I was able to work strategically along very clear goals and guided by clear behavioural values'. He champions the free market and keeping government out of the economy. However, he also encourages those below him to be 'looking not just at customers but actually looking at people and society and their lives'. Asked about remedying the bad behaviour of banks and other industry sectors, his answers relate to morality: 'you're not going to change those by regulation. In fact, you shouldn't. You'd change it by normative values in society. That's the best hope you've got, you know. By societal norms, by value systems.'

However, Tesco's record on truth and trust was not especially inspiring under Leahy. He initially made an impact by setting up the first supermarket loyalty card system, Tesco Clubcard, in 1993. Promoted as a reward scheme for regular customers, its other, more illicit aim was to gather marketing data on individuals (a model for today's online consumer tracking). Tesco also spent years manipulating accounting data to make its profits look better. Within a year of Leahy leaving, Tesco began issuing the first of many profit warnings as market share began diving. In 2017, after a three-year investigation, it had to pay out £235 million in fines, compensation and legal costs.

One of the ways the company had been fixing the accounts was by withholding payments and squeezing its many smaller suppliers. Coincidentally, I talked to one of these supplier CEOs at the time the accounting scandal became news. 'One of the nastiest companies we ever dealt with', he suddenly said. He then recounted his experience during a period when Leahy was very much in charge:

> Perhaps, four or five years ago, we did a promotion with Tesco for their Clubcard ... they were monthly settlements, and then in June they suddenly wouldn't pay. They waited until they owed us over half a million and then they paid, without any apology, no interest, nothing. And I suspect that if we'd gone to the wall they wouldn't have paid us anything.

I never doubted that Leahy believed in his moral code. But it seemed that he could effortlessly supress it, like a past traumatic memory, as and when it suited. He was not the only one.

Several business leaders voiced their concern with the environment and sustainability. Some, such as Neil Carson of Johnson Matthey or Peter Simpson of Anglian Water, responded by changing their company practices and products quite fundamentally. Others just seemed to believe in their own greenwash. Samir Brikho, AMEC's CEO, sounded very preoccupied with the environment. He used the E word 14 times. 'The environment is very close to my heart', he said, and 'I would love to give my children a better chance than I had and that includes the environment'. To that end he made sure his operations always considered environmental issues. The problem was that he was head of AMEC, a construction engineering company which made most of its profits working for big fossil fuel extractors. He ended his explanation with one of the ways AMEC did its bit with an example in his own office: 'there is a box down there. I have a switch there. As soon as I leave my office I push one switch and everything goes off in my office, because I don't need it … And if every one of us can do that, we'd be able to cut down on our carbon footprint now.'

Stephen Rubin OBE is Chairman of the Pentland Group, a company that began as a shoemaker and ended up as a sports brand investor and promoter. Pentland is sort of a posh Sports Direct. Rubin flits between contrary ethical and political positions, frequently trying to reconcile his views and practices. He supports the NHS and looking after the frail and sick, but also thinks it can't all be paid for, and the UK must compete better with the minimal welfare state economies of Asia. He dislikes the British 'politics of envy' and thinks a 'strong work ethic' should be rewarded, yet also practices Trump-style nepotism, appointing his son as CEO and his daughters to his executive board. The Rubin family comes 52nd on the 2017 *Sunday Times* Rich List.

His attempts to reconcile his worker-friendly ideas with his desire to be competitive leads him down an ethical rabbit hole. He rues the loss of the once proud textile industries of the North, and Pentland has just sponsored attempts to develop a new textiles centre in Manchester. But the company itself has been outsourcing all its own textile production abroad for decades. He talks of the company's 'very strong sense of corporate responsibility' and how this is applied in his UK offices and factories abroad. He concludes: 'people actually are very happy … we have, I think, a very, very loyal group, a good group of staff really.' But, as the conversation moves on, his sense of competition takes over:

> I was brought up to admire the work ethic, let's put it that way, which I think is important. I mean, in our offices as such, we don't pay overtime but you would see people there, if they've got a job to do. You'd see them there early, late or whatever it is … we've got a lot of women who might do three days a week or something because they've got kids at home. You find that these people are not doing three days, they're probably doing four or five days, because they want to do the right thing … in a real world you've got to compete.

Everyone talks about Asia. I always say when you've got to compete with the United States of America, where you've got places with instant dismissal, low costs, etc. And so, one has to be realistic.

In each of these examples, it was clear that the business leader had a strong moral code: trust and truth, environmental preservation, employment ideals and family values. Their leadership was undoubtedly preferable to that of, say, Philip Green, Tony Hayward or Mike Ashley. However, it was also clear that their values and business aims frequently didn't coincide. A large dose of self-deception was required to bridge the gap.

Institutionalised secrets and lies

If individuals operate with a certain degree of self-deception, then larger elite networks and professions appear almost entirely engineered towards keeping secrets. Denial and obfuscation are daily practices, learned and internalised.

Whitehall is one such example. The official line is that civil servants serve ministers by generating the evidence base to inform policy. They consult with an array of outside stakeholders on the way to turning policy into something tangible. Further public consultations and audits ensure democratic accountability.

However, exploring the government's bureaucratic machine suggests real practices are different. Parliament may have been opened up to scrutiny but Whitehall still prefers to operate in the shadows. Powerful civil servants are rarely in the public eye. Most will only be interviewed anonymously. Information release is tightly controlled. Departments can be very inward-looking and reluctant to go beyond particular favoured expert networks.[4]

At one point, I spent some time talking to civil servants about how evidence gathering and public consultations worked. Several sounded genuinely enthusiastic about engaging with the public but also revealed low expectations in this regard. Departments of State and parliamentary select committees were overflowing with experts and organised stakeholders. The wider public had neither the expertise nor concern necessary to participate. There was a natural source hierarchy, meaning Joe Public's contributions usually didn't make the cut.

As Sir David Normington, Permanent Secretary of the Home Office, explained: 'if you are not in the network you're not likely to be invited in. And how do you get into the consultation network? Well, it's a bit of chance. It's who you know.' One senior parliamentary clerk, in charge of trying to expand public involvement using online tools, suddenly dropped his official positive line. He said in a hushed tone:

> I don't want to sound negative, and don't quote me exactly on this, but … What is not yet clear is how much substance, either of material or of involvement, they bring to an inquiry, because they cost quite a lot in staff time and setting up … I'm not sure that, as it were, the general public engages at that level.

I got a blunter insight still when talking to Sir David Rowlands, who had worked in several departments in the civil service for over 30 years. He had been Permanent Secretary at the Department of Transport for some time, and was now only a few months from retirement. This explained his rather frank account of how public consultations really operated. Asked about evidence gathering to explore a new ministerial initiative, the answer came back:

> What makes you think ministers want evidence to support a new policy idea, as opposed to their policy idea? I've known lots of ministers who didn't … do not assume politicians always want evidence to support a policy position. They want it because it supports the political ideology.

As he explained, policy and evidence gathering was more often driven by political imperatives and the need to balance key interests. He went on to describe the process in relation to a recent road-pricing consultation. The department had set up a steering committee with carefully selected stakeholders, run outside of the department. This gave a pretence of 'independence' and wider stakeholder interest (and also allowed the minister to disown proposals if required). The actual consultation was similarly stage-managed:

> The least interesting part is the formal consultation itself; i.e., pulling out a consultation document and allowing twelve weeks for views and then sort of taking all that back to ministers and deciding what

the outcome is. Why do I say that? Well because many a consultation has already decided the outcome by the time you get to the formal public stage ... I mean that's not how the Department's basically operated. It's usually operating on a basis you've a pretty shrewd idea of what the outcome of this should be. And for most consultations in the earlier stages, it's how do you get to the point where you've actually kind of decided what it is you wish to consult upon?

Over the years, a whole set of professions have evolved to help keep institutional secrets. Their public remit is usually to improve communication, accountability and transparency. But their actual function is frequently to do the opposite.

One of these is the public relations and public affairs industry. The sector has spent many years trying to distance itself from its propaganda past and embrace its public communication function. Its professional associations and textbooks define the profession as a facilitator of clear two-way communication. Currently, the Chartered Institute of Public Relations gives its definition of PR as: 'the planned and sustained effort to establish and maintain goodwill and mutual understanding between an organisation and its publics'.[5]

However, in every elite network I have explored, it seems to be deployed as much to keep out or confuse the public as to inform it. Tim Blythe said: 'I had ten years in Whitehall, and 70% of press relations there was keeping stuff out of the papers.' Charles Lewington, who ran John Major's communications at Number 10, estimated that 'about 75%' of his efforts involved preventing bad news from getting out.

Things were the same in the commercial sector. Nick Chaloner, a corporate affairs director at Abbey National and Hill and Knowlton, explained: 'There are negative stories that we try to keep out of the press on a daily basis ... There are so many rumours and so much bar room talk.' Richard Oldworth, CEO of the consultancy Buchanan, stated: 'a lot of our job is to minimise bad news coverage. We get quite a lot of that. We often get calls on a Friday night from a Sunday journalist asking about a negative report and we try and get the article scrapped.'

And burying bad news is only one function of that side of the profession. The figureheads of the industry, from Edward Bernays to Lord Tim Bell,[6] have been inventing fake news, fake organisations and fake campaign groups for over a century.[7]

Accountancy is another such profession that conceals rather than enlightens. Professional bodies, firms and texts are big on things like transparency and trust. The 'mission' of the IFRS foundation[8] 'is to develop IFRS Standards that bring transparency, accountability and efficiency to financial markets around the world. Our work serves the public interest by fostering trust, growth and long-term financial stability in the global economy.' Go to one of the big four accountancy firms (PwC, EY, Deloitte, KPMG) and they plaster such terms across their websites. They offer reports and advice on good corporate governance, sustainability and codes of conduct.

But once again, the reality is different. Basic accounting and auditing is bread and butter but firms gain bigger and more lucrative contracts by manipulating financial data, as and when required, and creating tax avoidance schemes. One FTSE 100 CEO, a former accountant, boasted to me: 'Any idiot can get a 12-month result ... Give me a balance sheet or short-term incentives, short-term sales, or a product, I'll change it for your assumptions. I'll get you a 12-month result. A piece of cake.' Another time, I researched a big, hostile takeover and wondered how the bid documents produced by the rival companies gave such different financial pictures. The chief financial officer of one explained:

> Any finance director worth his salt can move the profits, one way or another, between any given year by a factor of between 5 and 10% ... there is huge scope to move profits around in an accounting sense. It is very difficult, almost impossible, for an outsider to get inside the accounts to check. Then there are market stats and you can make any company look good or bad if you pick the dates right.

The same big four accountancy firms are implicated in financial scandals on an almost annual basis. But their activities are rarely scrutinised by any part of the British Establishment because their influence spreads right across it. And, of course, they have facilitated tax evasion and avoidance schemes which have resulted in trillions of dollars being hidden across the world.[9]

Part of keeping on top for elites requires the formalising of double-talk at an institutional level. Information is really about misinformation. Engagement means disengagement. Greater transparency leads to more mystification.

The great lies of neoliberalism

In many accounts of power, those on top maintain their positions through forms of ideological domination.[10] Those who control the means of material production also control mental production. Although, as *The Dominant Ideology Thesis*[11] argued, ideologies often do more to hold elites together. Whether manipulating publics or unifying disparate groups of leaders, self-serving elite ideologies are everywhere.

The predominant elite ideology of recent decades is neoliberalism. This is both a political project and a broader set of ideas and values such as individualism, laissez faire, free choice and free markets.[12] A core component of neoliberalism is neoclassical economics. This has underpinned a series of economic policies and regulatory structures which have benefitted elites: lower taxes and market deregulation; monetarist policy levers over fiscal ones; privatisation; the marketisation of state functions; advancing globalisation and open trading borders; and weakening employee rights and welfare state provision.

If neoliberal political systems need an expert rationale for their activities, neoclassical economics normally provides it. So, if you want to cut taxes for the rich and for big corporations, there is the Laffer curve and supply-side economics. If you wish to defend cuts to government spending, there is the Rahn curve. If you need to justify the positive role of financial markets and the pay of financiers there is the Efficient Markets Hypothesis. If you feel a need to legitimise the growing power of central banks you turn to the Taylor Rule and the Great Moderation. And so on.

Many of these theories and ideas lack real empirical evidence to support them, or they rely on nonsensical logic.[13] All too often, they are built on abstract models and require the exclusion of real-world factors to work. In several cases, they are really just ideologies masquerading as objective realities. As Cathy O'Neil, the mathematician and critic of big data model abuses, says: 'Models are opinions embedded in mathematics'.[14] None of this, however, stops elites overtly referring to them to substantiate their decisions as and when required.

The bizarre thing is that many of those in power are highly sceptical too. They may defer to economists and economic rationales in public but in private they are aware things don't add up.

I found this a lot when interviewing financiers and when the subject of the EMH (Efficient Markets Hypothesis) came up. The EMH is the theory that provides the rationale for why financial markets always reach a natural equilibrium. Its thinking has determined the way modern financial markets are set up and regulated. Its original theorist, Eugene Fama, won the Nobel Prize in economics for it in 2013. This was a remarkable achievement considering that the financial crisis of 2007–8 proved just how wrong the theory was.

Most financiers believed that markets eventually reached the right price. But the theory they had studied at college didn't seem to apply to their experiences of real financial markets. 'It's a load of bollocks', said Andy Brough. Its logic suggested that there was no point in having professional fund managers, as no-one could outperform 'the market' in the long-run. As Michael Rimmer put it: 'If they are active fund managers they would find it hard professionally to believe in it. Like turkeys voting for Christmas.'

As Ralph Cox of Merrill Lynch concluded: 'If it were efficient you wouldn't get the massive share price swings that you see on a daily basis. We wouldn't be able to outperform versus other people.' But what really seemed problematic was the notion that everyone in markets operated rationally. Financiers knew that they and everyone else they dealt with weren't robots. As one explained: 'there are plenty of instances in recent history where we can demonstrate that investors are not being rational or profit-maximising individuals … the EMH does not adequately explain the serial irrationalities that take place in the market.'

In public, elites of all kinds refer to economist opinions as almost scientific facts. But in private, personal experience shows that too much of economics is too abstract for practical application.[15] As the former Chancellor Lord Lamont, a trained economist, said: 'I would say a degree in economics, it's useful as a way of thinking but it isn't really a practical tool for politics. And I'm extremely sceptical about economists frankly.' A top financier and former IMF economist told me: 'I think, off record, the whole thing is utterly disreputable. Competitive markets are not efficient markets. The academics have taken us all up the garden path and the practitioners have enjoyed making money from the whole thing.'

And Jeremy Goford, President of the Institute of Actuaries, said in an exasperated tone:

you will find it all over financial services, that competition does exactly the wrong thing … go and talk to the OFT[16] because they don't understand this more than most people don't understand this. Their economists think that competition is the best thing since sliced bread.

A key tool used for decision-making in business and politics is economic forecasting. Yet many of those who produced such forecasts thought the activity was entirely flawed. The former Labour Chancellor, Baron Alistair Darling, admitted: 'forecasting is simply the sum of all the assumptions you make, and if any of your assumptions are wrong it obviously changes your forecast.' George Osborne explained that his rationale for setting up the new Office for Budget Responsibility, was to stop the Treasury and Chancellor creating politically favourable forecasts for GDP and tax receipts: 'Because just slight changes to the assumptions of those can magically make your problems disappear.' The fund manager Edward Bonham Carter, explained that: 'if you spend 12 minutes a day trying to forecast the direction of the market you are probably wasting 11 minutes'. And Lord Norman Lamont said: 'I don't really believe in forecasting but I've never met anyone who's been chancellor who does believe in forecasting, you know. Lawson doesn't. Healey doesn't.'

Conclusion

Leadership is beset with contradictions and moral ambiguity. Doing the right thing for the organisation, employees and everyone else, while maintaining a top position, is hard. So leaders need secrets and lies to function. Many of these are for citizens and other stakeholders. But others are there to keep individual leaders themselves functioning. They are a way to justify difficult choices to oneself; to keep problems hidden, and difficult enquiring eyes out; and to maintain a flawed ideological framework for guiding everyday decisions and practices.

If capitalist democracy is predicated on ideals and theories that don't actually work in practice, then how does modern elite rule really operate? The answer, as the next chapter explains, is numbers.

Notes

1 Stated either in interview or on public record. See Aeron Davis (2017) 'Sustaining Corporate Class Consciousness Across the New *Liquid Managerial Elite* in Britain' in *British Journal of Sociology*, Vol. 68, No. 2, pp. 234–53.

2 For an account of how elite activities create inequality see Danny Dorling (2014) *Inequality and the 1%*, London: Verso.

3 Terry Leahy (2013) *Management in Ten Words*, London: Random House.

4 For an older but still very relevant account of Whitehall insularity, see David Marsh et al. (2001) *Changing Patterns of Governance in the United Kingdom*, Basingstoke: Palgrave.

5 www.cipr.co.UK; see also the most quoted book on the profession by James Grunig and Todd Hunt (1984) *Managing Public Relations*, New York: Holt, Rinehart and Winston.

6 Edward Bernays is regarded as the founder of modern PR in the US, setting up around the turn of the twentieth century. Lord Tim Bell has been a leading light in British political and corporate PR since the 1970s. Both also have documented histories of shady practices and questionable client lists.

7 For a fuller account of the industry's murky past and continuing shady practices see S. Ewen (1996) *PR! A Social History of Spin*, New York, Basic Books; David Miller and Will Dinan (2008) *A Century of Spin: How Public Relations Became the Cutting Edge of Corporate Power*, London: Pluto Press.

8 IFRS is the International Financial Reporting Standards foundation which sets international accounting standards.

9 See, for example, Nicholas Shaxon (2012) *Treasure Islands: Tax Havens and the Men Who Stole the World*, London: Vintage; and the Tax Justice Network site at: https://www.taxjustice.net/.

10 See, for example (1988) *An Antonio Gramsci Reader: Selected Writings 1916–1935*, ed. David Forgacs, London: Lawrence and Wishart; or Louis Althusser (1984) *Essays on Ideology*, London: Verso.

11 Nicholas Abercrombie et al. (1980) *The Dominant Ideology Thesis*, London: Allen and Unwin.

12 See accounts in David Harvey (2007) *A Brief History of Neoliberalism*, Oxford: Oxford University Press; or P. Mirowski and D. Plehwe eds (2009) *The Road to Mont Pelerin: The Making of the Neoliberal Thought Collective*, Cambridge, Mass.: Harvard University Press.

13 See Ha Joon Chang (2010) *23 Things They Don't Tell You About Capitalism*, London: Penguin; Steve Keen (2011) *Debunking Economics*, 2nd edn, London: Zed Books; or John Quiggin (2012) *Zombie Economics*, New Jersey: Princeton University Press.

14 See Cathy O'Neil's wide-ranging critique of the abuse of big data models, which is equally applicable to economic models, in her 2016 book: *Weapons of Math Destruction: How Big Data Increases Inequality and Threatens Democracy*, London: Penguin.
15 See this point well made in Joe Earle et al. (2016) *The Econocracy: The Perils of Leaving Economics to the Experts*, Manchester: Manchester University Press.
16 OFT was the Office of Fair Trading, running from 1973 to 2014. Now part of the Financial Conduct Authority.

7 The numbers game

Introduction

Today, everyone's lives appear to be increasingly linked to numbers and targets. Once, they were just an essential element of private commerce: sales, clients, billable hours and deadlines all make good targets. Then, teachers, doctors and other public-sector workers began working to the target. And now, our everyday consumption and social lives are measured and valued in clicks.

There are lots of reasons given for why human life seems to be increasingly reduced to a series of digits: capitalism, financialisation, public accountability. There is another which sounds rather more mundane. We have them because leaders don't know how else to lead.

If the liberal ideals of democracy don't really function in 'actually existing democracies',[1] if the grand theories of economics and business are too abstract, there are always numbers and targets instead. These become workable proxies for ideas and policies. They are the way leaders evaluate each other. They are how twenty-first-century *econocracy*[2] functions.

The problem is, in the virtual reality game that leadership has become, elites are both game creators and game players. They help set the targets by which they and everyone else are to be evaluated. They also agree the measures used and accounting tools deployed. If top people miscalculate and set themselves difficult targets, they can always game the system. Thus targets (or proxy targets for achieving something abstract) are imposed bluntly on those below, while being deftly avoided at the top.

Precarity and polyarchy

One of the things that slowly became clear to me when interviewing elites is that leaders always have another leader to defer to. Quite apart from the judgements of the amorphous mass of consumer-citizens, those at the top are constantly aware of being assessed by other elite figures. At least that's how they see it.

FTSE 100 CEOs appear to sit at the top of the pile when it comes to managing the economy. They are often in charge of hundreds of thousands of employees and billions of pounds. But corporate bosses know that they have bosses too. These are usually a select few big shareholders.

Most 'captains of industry' see themselves as hired employees, temporary incumbents of the top post. If things are not going according to plan, the board and chairman will convey shareholder displeasure. The CEO will be pointed in the direction of a sword to fall on. That threat is ever-present. William Claxton-Smith of Insight Investments explained: 'One of the big changes in corporate governance practice is that contracts longer than a year are now exceptionally frowned upon by investors.' Paul Walsh, who survived as CEO at Diageo for an impressive 12 years, said:

> Things have changed markedly over the last decade. You know, I think when I returned from the US I had a three-year contract, then it went to two-year and then it went to one-year. A rolling one-year contract I think when I cease to be Chief Executive … I think most people have gone to that. Now at the end of the day a CEO position is a high-risk position.

But, talking to top financiers, it soon became clear that the 'masters of the universe' had masters too. They managed billions as well and were often better paid than top CEOs. But they also had to persuade those with money, from big pension funds to the super-rich, to employ them. And, as I discovered, there was a whole sub-industry of specialists whose main preoccupation was evaluating fund managers. Poor performing financiers can lose their funds and positions very quickly. Even in good times, big City companies will carry out an annual cull of employees.[3]

Political and civil service elites also have their own sense of precarity and their own array of masters, real and imaginary. The average length of service for an MP in 2015 was 8.7 years, with a large proportion only lasting one term. The average tenure for a minister, which was never very long, has dropped below two years this century. Sam Coates, *The Times* lobby journalist, said: 'everybody's obsessed with their own futures and I think almost 80% of conversations will, however, indirectly, relate back to that.'

At the higher government levels, there is also an awareness of how international political and business elites are evaluating national performance. Global institutions and think tanks, such as the OECD, UN or World Bank, judge nations on an increasingly diverse set of comparisons: life expectancy, PISA education rankings,[4] national debt levels, ease of doing business, health outcomes, sustainability, productivity, happiness, trust in institutions, gold medals, and so on.

For the Conservative Party and Treasury, economic management for decades has been all about persuading the international community to come to the UK. Lord Cecil Parkinson explained this was the rationale for financial deregulation ('Big Bang') in the 1980s: 'We wanted the big players to come into our market if we were going to compete with Wall Street ... so it wasn't an accident that they came, it was opened up so that they would.'

In 1997, New Labour had a similar approach to achieving power and managing the economy. They had to persuade a range of international captains' of industry and the City, not to mention the press, that they were fit to govern. So, Labour's famed prawn cocktail offensive was rolled out. As the Labour minister Stephen Byers explained:

> We wanted to have a tax climate which was sort of attractive for international companies to come to the UK. We wanted to have a City which was not overregulated but had the freedom to grow ... a lot of it was about demonstrating how we felt we had to act to show our economic credibility.

After 2010, George Osborne repeatedly justified austerity, lower corporation taxes and deregulation on the basis that he had to convince the international credit ratings agencies and big business that Britain was still worth investing in. He set out his broader aims to me as Chancellor:

> The essential environment you want to create is one in which businesses want to invest and create jobs in a world where capital is highly

mobile, and very sought-after people are highly mobile. So you have to attract business to these shores. And I went out of my way to pick up the phone to get companies to move their headquarters here, as well as creating an environment in which they might want to, like reducing corporation tax.

In turn, every top CEO and financier who was asked about the social and economic state of the UK had an opinion on its merits relative to other nations. Sir Ian Cheshire, head of B&Q, gave me a detailed run-down of the social and economic conditions around the world:

Developing countries are emerging and growing at quite high rates. The China 8% GDP type place. So, it is extremely difficult for a UK-based economy to maintain its share of world trade, world exports, etc ... Germany's got a cultural base around business, which is not just the Mittelstand, but in the approach to work, business, training, education. There is a sort of glue. You see it in other places like Singapore or Korea ... By contrast the biggest single problem for France at the moment is the lack of labour market flexibility. And that is slowly killing the competitiveness. Ultimately, this all comes back to your international capability to compete.

This picture of leader competition, accountability and circulation is a form of what the political theorists Robert Dahl and Charles Lindblom referred to as polyarchy (or later, deformed polyarchy).[5] Such a system means elites always hold dominant positions in capitalist democracies. But they balance each other out and, if not responsive enough to the wider population, risk losing their positions.

In many ways, it also resembles the elite ideal view of how leadership should operate. Those at the top believe they got there on merit, having succeeded through a fair competition with others. It is part of the great modern meritocracy myth.[6]

In such a system, the larger public has a say, direct or indirect, on who leads. But the list of potential leaders to choose from is decided by elites themselves. The question then becomes: how are leaders assessed and selected by other leaders?

Although elite leadership selections may be influenced by self-interest, it is no longer a matter of simply choosing someone else from the same old-boys' club. Likewise, it is harder to base leader choices on the merits of an individual's ideas, creativity or expertise.

Elites rarely possess real expertise. For every innovative CEO, there are many more bosses with superior accounting skills and little imagination. For each visionary statesperson, there are many more dexterous networkers and seller politicians.

But there is another problem too. Once in power, big ideas and public rhetoric do not simply translate into decision-making. Grand theories about democracy and markets are no more than abstract ideals. They offer no real-world guide or basis for leader evaluation.

What is more practicable, for those with ruthless rationality but few ideas and little imagination, is numbers and targets.

Replacing ideas with numbers

In the business and financial world, regardless of the shine of the CEO or the dazzle of their ideas,[7] the bottom line always comes down to the numbers. Every new business leader has to have them to impress their investors. For decades business strategies have been broken down into metrics and targets, with the most important target being the share price. Neil Carson, after ten good years at Johnson Matthey, was a veteran of the numbers game: 'The top of the list on the sustainability 2017 targets was double earnings per share. And the second one was, we're going to halve the raw materials used per unit output ... and you need to get a 20% return on capital expenditure investment.'

Mark Wilson, the new CEO of Aviva, was all about the metrics: metrics to persuade his investors, and metrics to guide his management team:

> You've got to have the key metrics. In Aviva ... there were no metrics and there was no strategy ... My strategy here is I've got the investment thesis, which I launched in March. That's very simple. And it's got five key metrics ... Recently, I had a cell review day. I got the business unit heads of these cells in, all in the room together, and ... I ranked them on the five key metrics.

For their part, financiers jumped at the chance to add a new set of metrological targets to their evaluation models. As the financial analyst Michael Levy put it: 'Everybody loves ratings and tables and rankings and all the rest of it. If you tried hard you could probably rate almost anything about large companies.' And, in turn, the investment consultant Nick Fitzpatrick, quantified his fund managers: 'We do have a template of seven or eight criteria against which we assess how well a fund manager is doing against those criteria, and then we end up with a rating.'

Such management and evaluation methods slowly found their way into government, as the neoliberal agenda was rolled out after 1979. Several others have documented how such ideas and practices became central to the reorganisation of the British regulatory state.[8] Key elements of this included extensive auditing and New Public Management.[9] In each case, management practices that had developed in the financial sector, including targets and audits, were adopted across Westminster and Whitehall.

But, while interviewing ministers and civil servants, it became apparent that such activities were not simply applied downwards to manage civil servants and public-sector employees. They had two other uses for elites. First, they were a means of transforming the grandiose ideas and rhetoric of politicians into meaningful activities. Second, they then became an evaluative tool; a way by which elite performance could be judged, and successes claimed.

I realised how this shift had taken place in the early years of the new Thatcher administration. It was during this time that Keynesianism was dumped and monetarism adopted as part of the emerging neoliberal economic consensus. I talked to several civil servants and advisors who were part of this transformation. One of these was Lord Terry Burns, a key advisor who went on to become Permanent Secretary of the Treasury.

Burns was an economist who loved creating models and had worked for years with others developing an alternative model of the UK economy. During the 1970s economic crisis his ideas got quite a bit of news coverage. Since he appeared to offer something more compatible with Thatcherism, he was brought into the Treasury to turn the new theory into something more applied:

we started promoting the idea of a medium-term financial strategy, and we integrated the whole exchange rate sort of thing, and the impact of money on the exchange rate into the model ... I think they hired me for two things: one was that they thought my views were broadly sympathetic with what they were seeking to do, in terms of

control of public sector deficits, monetary control. But also because
I had done all this model building.

In early 1980, the grand 'medium-term financial strategy' was
launched. But the already struggling economy then crashed badly.
Eventually things stabilised, and inflation and unemployment began
to drop. But while the new economic paradigm was being lauded,
in the background many specific elements of the official strategy
were discredited and quietly dropped. Regardless, Lord Burns felt
his theories and models had been proved right by the economy's
upturn. But he was unable to explain the flaws in the theory or
why the real economy often didn't behave as the model predicted:

> Well there was a monetary model and there was a kind of real model.
> There was a model of the monetary side of the economy, and there
> was another model of the real side of the economy ... but if you
> look at the next 25 to 30 years, until we ran into the crisis of 2007,
> it worked out I would say reasonably well.

Burns was also unable to account for the unpredicted financial
shocks that kept coming. These weren't in his models. So he referred
to them as 'great squalls', like they were some unforeseen act of
God. Seeing I looked unconvinced, he had another go. It worked
because they managed to reduce the theory to some concrete targets.
And the targets seemed to work: 'we moved gradually to looking at
a portfolio of monetary condition measures. And a basic principle
was that you would get down the inflation rate, and growth would
be established by getting your budget deficit under control.'

Burns was really saying that if you manage to get key economic
indicators to follow the targets in the model, the policy will all work
out in the end ... somehow. Working out in the end turned out to
be hitting a target for inflation. During another conversation, Sir
John Gieve put it rather more bluntly. Inflation targeting, almost by
accident, became the defining proxy for the new economic paradigm:

> out of this mess of the medium-term financial strategy, monetary
> targeting, exchange rate targeting, we finally latched on to inflation
> targeting around '92, when we were forced out of the ERM. And the
> power of that idea then sort of slowly grew and dominated economic
> policymaking right up to 2007. Arguably it still does.

The game of target-based economic policy became more refined during the New Labour years. Behind Gordon Brown's 'golden rules', 'no return to boom and bust' and 'post-neoclassical endogenous growth theory', something else was happening. The new target culture was taking over everywhere. Vicky Pryce was a top economic advisor, eventually becoming joint head of the Government Economic Services. She explained everything to me:

> The Labour Party Manifesto used to be translated into a number of Public Service Agreements. So there were all these targets, things that had to be met over a number of years in individual areas that they wanted to select. Child poverty, education, environmental stuff, blah-blah … PSAs were then reduced from hundreds to just 30. So there would be a crime, sort of justice, PSA with some subheadings of course in each case … I was the person responsible for PSA number one, productivity for the UK economy. So we'd bring in lots of people, and we would measure our productivity … There was a whole system devised by the Treasury. There was a group there that actually gave us sort of red lines, or amber or green depending on how well we were doing.

Without anyone quite noticing, the target-driven tails began wagging the dogs. Today, it does not really matter if a CEO is innovating or creating a healthy company with long-term growth prospects. It only matters that the numbers and targets associated with the strategy are being hit. If that happens, the most important target, the share price, goes up.

In the public sector, it doesn't matter whether health outcomes or school education levels are improving. It only matters that the targets that equate to success are being reached. If productivity rises because working hours have edged up, if more people are seen in A&E within four hours, or more nine-year-olds can spot a fronted adverbial, leaders have succeeded.

In the same way, it doesn't matter if financial market theory is illogical, if monetarism is fatally flawed, if there is a new economy, or somewhere in the North of England a powerhouse of marching makers exists. What matters is that the ideas can be linked to a series of metrological targets. Get the numbers to fit and the models are proved right. Hit the targets and the theory is vindicated. Leaders are doing their job and can be rewarded accordingly.

And while those in charge are proclaiming their target-striking prowess, it is everyone below who is now directed towards hitting their own targets to make *the* targets work. For ordinary people, everyday lives can change quite substantially. But, for those at the top, it's all just one virtual reality game of numbers.

Gaming the system

Although numerical targets are more defined and measurable than general theories and grandiose rhetoric, they are also malleable. Elites are well-positioned to influence their construction for two obvious reasons.

First, they increasingly possess the economics and accounting knowledge necessary to understand how they are devised and selected. Financiers obviously know numbers more than they know anything else. But other leadership sectors are increasingly numbers-oriented too. In a 2014 audit, three quarters of FTSE 100 CEOs had a qualification requiring more advanced numeracy skills, such as in economics or accounting. Three quarters of permanent secretaries either had an economics degree or had previously worked in the Treasury or financial sector. And 19 of 45 front bench politicians had studied economics, usually through their PPE degree.[10]

Second, these same elites are often part of the negotiation and construction of auditable targets which are then used to evaluate their future selves. That includes a say on the choice of metrics, the accounting tools and the time periods used in the appraisal process. In other words, they get to be the game player while also being able to set the rules of the game. And they often pick the referee too. And, if they are inept enough to still mess things up, they get to change the rules half way through.[11]

This became quite obvious when talking to CEOs about the secrets of their success. For James Hill, CEO of the Findus Group: 'it's a very important thing in leadership to be conscious of how you are defining success and to make sure that that is, in a sense, achievable ... and it is surprising how much scope, how much latitude you have to define success in your own terms.'

For Mark Wilson of Aviva, his chosen metrics were part of a strategic plan. They were selected, along with other bits of information, to manage the expectations of his investors:

we focused all those shareholders on five things. That's it, because shareholders will focus on what you ask them to focus on and what you keep on talking to them about. So it's simple. And you want problems. You highlight the problems. I've always highlighted problems. You say: 'These are our problems.' Then you fix them. They'll reward you for it in your stock price ... you just need to align with the same metrics that you're giving the shareholders.

No CEO admitted quite to gaming their own system. But many let slip that it could be done and that others obviously did it. And, in turn, investors found themselves trying to see through what was happening. The dialogues between the two had evolved into a complex game of cat and mouse. As Michael Rimmer of Investec Asset Management explained:

> The company might look fabulous in terms of the trend in earnings, 10% this year, 20% next year, etc. But if you look at them closely they have never actually made a positive cash flow return on investment in their entire history. They are just value-destroying machines.

Government ministers and top mandarins are equally capable of gaming their own systems. Under Mrs Thatcher, Treasury officials became skilled at accounting reclassification techniques, to make sure budget targets such as the PSBR were hit.[12] Former civil servants explained how the 'rules' were recast as required. Sir John Gieve gave such an account of Nigel Lawson's abilities here:

> I remember going to the IMF in, I guess '88, and Lawson made a speech which argued that you shouldn't look at the current account deficit as significant on its own. You had to look at the capital account because the current account was balanced by the capital account ... And looking back on it, this was a classic ex-post justification for the fact that we had a big current account deficit.

By the time New Labour reached office, figure fiddling was becoming de rigueur. Out of the monetarist mash-up of Lord Burns' time, New Labour ran with the inflation-targeting policy. They handed the task to the newly independent Bank of England but that didn't stop them fiddling with the figures, including how inflation itself was calculated or how the health of government accounts was gauged.[13]

Baron Andrew Turnbull, who headed the civil service at the time, was scathing as he looked back on the way key economic policy indicators were shifted:

> we made the silly move, from the RPI to the CPI.[14] And the reason we did was because in 2003 we had the five tests verdict. Brown wanted to be able to demonstrate that we were nearly there ... he said: 'we're taking steps that will kind of be preparatory to that', and one of them was 'let's adopt the measure of inflation that they use' ... it looked as though our financial position was actually rather good ... the Brown/Balls mantra was balance across the cycle. But you kept redefining the cycle in ways that were beneficial to you.

This gaming of systems is why leaders can keep getting rewarded even though their perceived success is a mirage. It's why bankers have kept paying their employees billions in bonuses even as states were bailing those same banks out during the financial crisis. It's why corporate heads get rewarded for take-overs even though most studies show that the majority of such acquisitions are loss-making in the long-term. And it's why CEO pay has continued to rise considerably faster than levels of productivity, share prices or average earnings. Between 2010 and 2015, FTSE 100 CEOs went from earning 120 times average salary to 183 times.[15]

Such gaming also means governments can claim that the economy is doing well when, for many people, it isn't. In the latter years of the coalition government, George Osborne and others declared that the economy was no longer in crisis and was on the way to recovery. The official figures showed that inflation was under control, unemployment was declining and GDP was rising.

Yet this picture had no basis in reality for many people. The CPI inflation figure used did not include changes to house prices or rental costs, which have been rising way above inflation (averaging 6.9% per year since 1980). The employment figures did not account for the rapid growth of temporary, insecure and zero-hours contracts. By the start of 2017, such employment had risen to three million, or one in ten of the workforce. National GDP rises were not quoted in per capita terms, and did not show the huge regional differences that existed. They also did not reveal that ordinary incomes had been stagnating in real terms since the crisis (and long before that in many places and occupations). In fact, between 2007 and 2015, the UK was about the only mature economy to record both an increase in GDP and a fall in real wages.[16]

2016 was the year these huge differences in elite economic perception and non-elite experience became suddenly clear. Those parts of the UK with the strongest leave votes in the EU referendum were also the ones where local economic conditions had become most dire. Just as the Tory Party Brexiteers developed some misguided idea of Britain's place in the world, so the metropolitan elite remainers had little idea about the true state of the real economy for many people. Those in the better-off South East had spent too much time listening to the gamed version of the economy produced by 'experts'. Even Michael Gove, like a stopped clock, can be right on occasion.

Conclusion

Today's leaders do not just manage those lower down through numbers and targets. They manage themselves, their elite peers and rivals this way too. It's easier than evaluating creativity, innovation and well-being; especially when they have few of these qualities themselves.

But it also means that leadership has been turned into a virtual reality game, where elites get to both design the game and play it. In this game, leaders have special powers and can use these to keep accumulating treasures and more powers. But everyone else far below just becomes another powerless, mass blur of zeros and ones.

Of course, leaders can't keep on top for ever. New game players with advanced skills are always waiting in the wings. So those at the top need to develop their exit strategies. That takes us on to Part IV.

Notes

1 A phrase coined by Nancy Fraser (1990) 'Rethinking the Public Sphere: A Contribution to the Critique of Actually Existing Democracy' in *Social Text*, No. 25/6, pp. 56–80.

2 See Aeron Davis (2017) 'The New Professional Econocracy and the Maintenance of Elite Power' in *Political Studies*, Vol. 65, No. 3, pp. 595–610; or Joe Earle et al. (2016), *The Econocracy: The Perils of Leaving Economics to the Experts*, Manchester: Manchester University Press.

3 See Joris Luyendijk (2015) *Swimming with Sharks: My Journey into the World of the Bankers*, London: Guardian Books.

4 OECD: Organisation for Economic Co-operation and Development; PISA: Programme for International Student Assesment.

5 Dahl and Lindblom's original work was published in 1953. A fuller overview of polyarchy is in Dahl's (1989) *Democracy and its Critics*, New Haven: Yale University Press.

6 There are a number of books pulling apart the myth of meritocracy. See a recent account by Jo Littler (2017) *Against Meritocracy: Culture, Power and Myths of Mobility*, London: Routledge.

7 For an account of how CEOs combine stories and figures see Julie Froud et al. (2006) *Financialization and Strategy: Narratives and Numbers*, London: Routledge.

8 See Michael Moran (2003) *The British Regulatory State*, Oxford: Oxford University Press.

9 See Michael Power (1997) *The Audit Society: Rituals of Verification*, Oxford: Oxford University Press; and Christopher Hood (1995) 'The "New Public Management" in the 1980s: Variations on a Theme' in *Accounting, Organizations and Society*, Vol. 20, No. 2/3, pp. 93–109.

10 See Aeron Davis (2017) 'The New Professional Econocracy and the Maintenance of Elite Power' in P*olitical Studies*, Vol. 65, No. 3, pp. 595–610.

11 Examples of business leaders succeeding by also setting market rules and standards are in Mark Granovetter and Patrick McGuire (1998) 'The Making of an Industry: Electricity in the United States' in Michel Callon, *The Laws of the Markets*, Oxford: Blackwell; and Don Slater (2002) 'Capturing Markets from the Economists' in Paul du Gay and Michael Pryke, *Cultural Economy*, London: Sage.

12 PSBR is Public Sector Borrowing Requirement. See Leo Pliatsky's insider account of how such things were manipulated in his (1989) *The Treasury Under Mrs Thatcher*, Oxford: Basil Blackwell.

13 See Simon Jenkins (2006) *Thatcher and Sons: A Revolution in Three Acts*, London: Penguin.

14 RPI and CPI are two ways of calculating inflation: Retail Price Index and Consumer Price Index. Both are malleable as they change according to what's included in the calculation.

15 See Ownership Commission (2012) *Plurality, Stewardship and Engagement*, London: Ownership Commission; George Cox (2013) *Cox Review: Overcoming Short-Termism within British Business: The Key to Sustained Economic Growth*, London: Labour Party; and annual reports at High Pay Centre.

16 See, in particular, Simon Wren-Lewis's blogs on the differences between media and real presentations of the economy, at https://mainlymacro.blogspot.co.uk/.

Part IV

EXIT STRATEGIES

8 The safety of the herd

Introduction

Leaders and leading appear to be inextricably linked terms. Leaders lead. They innovate. They take risks. They make tough decisions, especially when faced with a crisis. Others follow.

The trouble is that leaders and leading are not really that synonymous. For much of the time, elites follow more than they lead. Top journalists fear missing the big story of the day and monitor each other. MPs do what the party whip tells them. Ministers stick to collective cabinet responsibility. CEOs prefer to be fast followers rather than innovators and explorers. Financiers keep close to their index. No-one likes to strike out or do something too radical in case it all goes wrong big time. Individual risk is set against system or public risk, and personal risk usually comes first.

And when a real crisis hits, most leaders don't lead. They run to join the safety of the pack. Financiers huddle together while the banking system crashes around them. Politicians vote to support their leader's misguided ideas, whatever the consequences. Top bureaucrats call on the outside experts to tell them what to do. By such means, when the crisis is over, they all get to walk away with their bonuses and networks intact.

Playing it safe in business and finance

In every leadership sector I've explored, I've come to realise that a lot of everyday existence is about playing it safe. That means going with what everyone around you is doing. Quite often, there is a desire to try another approach or to go against common opinion.

But in most cases, the final decision made and the path chosen is more cautious. A personal risk-benefit calculation is made, and the follow-others-option usually makes more sense.

One way this became clear to me was when asking top CEOs to reflect on what it was about them and their business strategies that had brought them success. There were some common answers: determination, analytical ability, people management skills, team-building. The answer that stood out most was the one given by Francis Salway, CEO of Land Securities:

> You have to have the odd good idea. I think it's unrealistic to think that people are constantly having wonderful ideas. I once said to somebody, 'I don't expect to have a good idea more than once every three years.' And he said 'Francis, I had one good idea in my whole career, and it made my career.'

Salway's answer caught my attention because he was about the only top CEO to talk about ideas. A few talked about strategic vision. Fewer still talked about something different they did that really made a difference. Ideas and innovation were barely mentioned. Nor were they expected. Stephen Hester of RBS, when asked about innovation, said: 'If you're doing something different from everyone else, you have to say what is it that makes you think you're cleverer than them … It's a higher bar actually.'

Why was innovation or creativity so neglected? It all came down to risk. The 'risk' word figured highly in most business leaders' thinking. When asked about making big decisions, they soon began talking about 'risk evaluations', 'risk audits' and 'risk comparisons'. Doing something new or innovative was risky.[1] It usually involved a big investment in time and money. The breadth of market interest was not yet proven. And the worst risk of all was that it could affect the share price in the short-term. As one UK study found, 75% of managers would avoid new projects with long-term value creation if they were damaging to short-term earnings.[2]

For CEOs, there were a whole lot of other strategies to pursue which were less risky. There was the playing the numbers game (not usually divulged as being a strategy). Exploiting dominant market positions or developing micro monopolies was another. But, most often, growth came down to doing the same things better or in a more cost-efficient way. As Stephen Hester went on: 'Once in a while, you actually try and do something that is different from what anyone else is doing. And, once in a while you even succeed in that. But that is less often than simply trying to do similar things but a bit better.'

Lots of CEOs had come to this conclusion through personal experience. There were stories of wasted investments of tens or hundreds of millions, only to be beaten to market by a competitor. Or for a partner company to change the deal. Or for a new technology to make the old investment redundant. And, even if first, it wasn't long before another company copied your idea. 'Other people innovate, you respond', said Sir Ian Cheshire of B&Q. As he then explained: 'There's a really nice product innovation that's coming out in the spring for us at B&Q. We'll have a year probably where we'll have an exclusive on it. Then it'll get copied.'

For all these reasons, it was a lot easier to watch others and, if it worked, quickly jump on the bandwagon. Alan Parker of Whitbread reflected on his experiences:

> we went through a big investment in enterprise wide systems which, frankly, turned out to be not best in class for our various activities. And I would say from that experience ... I would definitely always want to see it working elsewhere. Rather than paying the price of being a leading-edge innovator, I'd much rather be a fast follower.

These CEOs were only confirming what J.M. Keynes had concluded about the business world back in the 1930s, which is that: 'it is better for reputation to fail conventionally than to succeed unconventionally'.[3] Keynes had a lot to say on this in relation to top financiers. In his experience, individuals made investment decisions less on the basis of their own opinion and more by second-guessing what the majority opinion of everyone else was. Stocks were only valuable if most others thought they were too.

Whether or not they had read Keynes, every financier in the London Stock Exchange I talked to was aware of the importance of watching other market players and movements. Each of them had the computing power and software to monitor every movement of securities, indexes and markets. And they all took Keynes' principles to heart. The end result was that people, although making independent decisions, acted like they were part of a pack. Rick Lacaille of State Street commented on the financial analysts he followed: 'you get herding amongst analysts because they don't want to feel exposed. They don't want to be the person who's downgrading a stock when everyone else is upgrading because career risk might be quite high.'

Nick Fitzpatrick saw something similar with pension fund trustees: 'There is a tendency of trustees to try and be the same as everybody else because they won't get criticised for that, which does mean that some of the appointments get a herd-like response.'

And John Rogers, CEO of the UK Society of Investment Professionals, concluded the following about his members:

> You've heard of the herd instinct. Over the last 10 years, by and large, there has not been much to choose between the approaches of the big managers ... If you pick different strategies you are either going to be top of the tree or at the bottom ... So, the moral of the story is that it's a lower risk strategy to follow the herd.

In all these cases, business 'leaders' do not lead. The daily default practice is to follow. Following is less risky than leading somewhere unknown and standing out from the crowd. Bigger organisations and bigger funds mean bigger risks. New technologies make both monitoring and copying of rivals easier. So herding is becoming more common not less.

Playing it safe at Westminster

Westminster is awash with fast followers and herds. This is particularly the case in political lobby journalism which has a lot in common with the financial world. Both sectors are driven by fast-moving fashions. And everyone wants to be in with the It Crowd.

In the journalists' case, the lobby provides the conditions in which reporters, although competitors, regularly move together as a pack. Their working conditions mean that correspondents from diverse media share offices and facilities. They have similar story inputs and frequent chances to exchange ideas. Nick Robinson, BBC Political Editor, explained how reporters came together:

> The fact that we're all in Westminster means that I spend more time with rival journalists from rival organisations than I do with fellow journalists from my own organisation ... If you're all in a room

asking questions of a politician, or a spokesman, quite often a mood emerges as to whether that person did it effectively, or didn't do it effectively, is in trouble, isn't in trouble, has answered the point or hasn't answered the point.

The same concerns about personal risk are there when it comes to setting news agendas and story lines. On the one hand, reporters want to get an exclusive or a scoop. On the other, even the most experienced of hacks are terrified of missing the story of the day. Peter Riddell, chief political correspondent of *The Times*, explained how and why reporting could be governed by personal issues of risk: 'it makes everyone risk averse, because the news desks go: "why haven't we got this story?" So, people are ensuring that they will cover something because someone else might have it.' Michael White, Political Editor of the *Guardian*, explained in more detail:

> It's what they call defensive filing ... you're looking at something which you gave a hundred words to, which is the lead in rival newspapers and the lead item on the *Today Programme* and then somebody says: 'Why did we fuck up?' ... you constantly have to anticipate, and you know, it's not a science. It's what other people do as well that matters, and whether that story is going to take off ... Sometimes the narrative is overwhelming and everybody follows it because it's the only thing to do. And you follow it whether you like it or not.

Politicians move in packs too. In Westminster, the biggest packs are the parties. Tight discipline is organised through the Whips' Office; a sort of modern-day Big Brother machine for monitoring politicians. Every misdeed, be it a wrong vote, poor TV appearance, bad tweet or illicit affair, is recorded and filed away. Lord John Wakeham, Chief Whip during Mrs Thatcher's second term, explained how it all worked: 'there is never a moment when Parliament is not sitting, when one of your junior whips is not sitting on the frontbench. He reports to you on every single speech ... it's called the dirt book. It's the notes that they make of everything for the Chief Whip, because it tells you anything.'

Most back-benchers rarely defy the dictates of the Whip's Office. On the front bench, ministers hold to the official line and stick to collective cabinet responsibility. Nick Raynsford, the Labour minister, put it simply: 'you have to accept, as a condition of going into government, collective responsibility ... if you feel very strongly about a particular issue then you have to leave.' And Lord John Thurso, on the Liberal Democrat front bench, explained:

> broadly speaking you do as you're told. We follow into the lobby like sheep in whichever direction the Whip's pointing us ... it's very rare that you decide suddenly at the last moment not to vote with the Whip on a subject, which, as a member of the Shadow Cabinet is quite a dire thing to do.

There are many moments when those at Westminster have to make choices between what they think is right and what their party or media outlet want. The larger the stakes the harder the choice. And most of the time, whether journalist or politician, the personal career-risk-analysis says follow the organisational line.

The decision to join the US assault on Iraq in 2003 was one of those times[4] when self-preservation meant ignoring evidence and rational thought. The key justification for the invasion was Iraq's WMD.[5] No substantiated evidence for their existence was ever given to the Cabinet or Parliament. The UN was unconvinced and refused to back action. The protest march in London was the biggest in UK history. A MORI survey in January found that 77% of the public opposed such action without UN support. As the Labour MP Glenda Jackson put it: 'I just don't know how intelligent people could buy into that because it was so patently not true.'

Yet at each stage, first the Cabinet, then the Commons and Press, came out in a clear majority to support the attack. Just three ministers resigned. A third of Labour MPs rebelled but, with Conservative Party support, the Labour government won two thirds of the overall vote. A content analysis of news content found that 89% of coverage 'assumed the probable existence' of WMD.[6]

I spoke to some 35 politicians and journalists there at the time. Many did not want to believe that the WMD threat had been entirely made up. Some simply believed that the brutal Hussein regime should be deposed anyway. But it was also clear that the Blair government and party apparatus had put extensive pressure on all concerned. They aggressively attacked the BBC and other reporters who questioned their crude 'dodgy dossiers'. As Jeremy Corbyn explained: 'over the Iraq war the pressures put on the media were absolutely extraordinary from the Ministry of Defence and Downing Street.' The journalist Peter Oborne described the collective view of the political lobby: 'Clearly the mood of the lobby was that they didn't want to confront Downing Street about the fact that they were being systematically misled … As a whole, they accepted it. There were some exceptions but among major columnists nobody really diverged.'

The stakes were also set very high for Labour MPs. In private, Blair threatened to resign and call a general election if he didn't get a Labour majority. Revolt became a greater personal risk, especially when it became obvious the government would win with Conservative support. Some MPs even admitted to joining the lobbying effort of doubters to prove their loyalty. Gary Gibbon, *Channel Four News*'s Political Editor, explained the transition:

> If the vote had gone the wrong way … not only would Tony Blair have had to resign … the government would have been humiliated internationally, shown to be unfit to govern because they tried to do something. They couldn't do it. It's the ERM times ten, Suez revisited. It would have been cataclysmic. And in the end, people like Gordon Brown realised that. And knew they had to come out and put their shoulders to the wheel whatever they thought in private.

The Tony Dye story

It was the Tony Dye story that really showed me just how hard leaders run for the safety of the herd in times of crisis. When I first heard the story, I was interviewing an experienced fund manager at his City offices. John Davies appeared very much as one might imagine a successful, experienced financier would. He had the smart City look. He spoke authoritatively, using technical jargon to explain how and why things happened in stock markets. There was a rational explanation for everything.

And then we got on to the subject of the dot-com boom and bust of 2000. From around the mid-1990s investors started pouring hundreds of billions into new internet start-ups. Most of these came to be worthless when the bust came. As Davies started to recall this time, his calm assurance vanished. He sounded alarmed and flustered, as if he was living through it again. Fund management no longer sounded rational:

> The conventional rules still apply. But nobody believes. There's always a reason. Yes, the company's making losses. Yes, there is a financing deficit. But the prospects are so good that by next year everything will be hunky-dory and tickety-boo ... It had got to that stage that the next issue from Goldman Sachs was going to come on at £1 and start trading at £2 and you couldn't afford not to have any. It really didn't matter what the company did.

Nothing made sense, but every professional investor was doing it. And then came that Tony Dye story. Tony Dye was one of the few fund managers who dared to say what many suspected in private. 'Dr Doom', as he came to be called, said it was all 'rubbish' and 'a bubble'. Dye wasn't just some oddball outlier. Davies called him 'the highest profile value analyst in the market'. His investment firm had been topping the performance list for several years. Dye stuck his neck out and paid for it with his job. Davies explained how and why not following the herd in buying dodgy internet stocks was a problem:

> What happens then, of course, is that people worry because they haven't got them. Because they are being measured against indices of things that contain representatives of these things. They feel they've got to be exposed to it. The odd investor who stood back from it, Tony Dye being the supreme example, actually gets the sack before he's proved right ... If you look at an index that doesn't do anything but 10% of it goes up in a year, the index would have gone up 10%. If you didn't have any exposure there you would have underperformed by 10%, even though it's relatively small. Most will forgive one year's performance, maybe two. But then by the third year you must have made a mistake.

Dye's mistake was not that he called the hi-tech bubble for what it was, but to call it a couple of years too early. He took all his funds out of hi-tech stocks. But because these were the ones making most money, his firm's relative performance dropped dramatically. Dye was then fired just weeks before he was proved right. The obvious point of the story was that no-one, not even the best investors, could have called the top of the new economy boom.

But after several more interviews, it seemed that there was a bit more to the story than that. Nine other financiers mentioned Tony Dye. His name came up whenever they were asked about the dot-com boom and why they kept buying in the face of all reason. Ten years later and other leaders, without prompting, also recalled the Dye story. Only this time the topic was the 2007–8 financial crash. Francis Salway, CEO of Land Securities, and Lord Terry Burns, then Chairman of Santander, both mentioned him in relation to difficult decision-making at the time. So did a senior Treasury official.

For all of them, the Tony Dye story had a wider resonance. It was a sort of Aesop's fable for financial elites everywhere. The moral soon became clear: in tough times, it's much better to do what everyone else is doing even if you think it's completely irrational and destructive. Then, if it goes wrong you can't be singled out for blame. But if you do something very different and it goes wrong, then you're a dead man walking. Thus the Tony Dye story gave them a moral justification for doing the wrong thing.

And somewhere deep down, most people knew it was the wrong thing, both in 2000 and 2007–8. Even if they were true financial market believers, even if they didn't know a crash was immanent, things just didn't add up. Standard accounting measures, historical trends and common sense were all wilfully ignored.

During the dot-com boom, the London Stock Exchange more than doubled in value in the five years up to 2000. That was far in excess of any previous historical measures, including just before the Wall Street Crash of 1929.[7] Priceline.com, an online company for selling excess airline capacity, came to be worth $150 billion, or more than the entire airline industry.[8] The same sense of defying financial gravity was evident in the lead-up to the 2007–8 financial crash. The derivatives market rose in value over a decade, from $15 trillion to $600 trillion, or close to 12 times total world GDP.[9] From 1995 to 2007, house prices went from four and a half times average earnings to nine times. And Northern Rock, the first bank to collapse, had loans worth over £100 billion but assets of only £1.5 billion.

It was also clear to some in the Treasury that things did not really add up either. Market values were out of kilter. Projections were wildly optimistic. But the economy was riding high and tax income from the City was proving very useful. Dan Corry, a senior economic advisor to New Labour, explained:

obviously, if you've got a sector that's doing really well and you can tax it, that's good news. And if the sector says: 'we could do even better if you made this change', then you go a bit soft ... some of the assumptions on the future growth of revenues was very dependent in retrospect on the City carrying on doing well. And a lot of turnover of houses and stamp duty. And you look back on that and you think 'Blimey, that was risky.'

Eventually, I did get to meet Tony Dye himself. He was everything the typical City fund manager was not: Northern, dour, simply dressed and straight-talking. He had recovered somewhat and was now running his own Dye Asset Management. But he remained bitter and contemptuous about the workings of high finance. In his view, truth and reason were continually overridden by the golden rule of the City – look out for number one:

> There's incredible sources and there's less credible sources but there's no credible sources at all. There is no-one out there who has really got your interests at heart ... You can't be too cynical or realistic about how the system works. It's out there to make money for those businesses, and money for those people, and the whole thing is the most sophisticated sales force in the world. But it's not out there to help investors make money. It's out there to take as much money from investors without them protesting.

Asked about the boom and bust of 2000, he had a variety of responses. 'It was complete mania. It was a fantasy that I can't explain' was his first reply. Then he moved on to behavioural finance to account for others' seemingly irrational activities. Finally, Tony Dye gave me his own version of the Tony Dye story, while also predicting the 2007–8 crash to come:[10]

> They go along with that because the incentives for not going along with it are not very pleasant. They don't give a shit about the long-term returns. They are interested in their business and their business is dependent on not underperforming indices in the short-run. With notable exceptions that's how it works. You don't want to piss against the wind ... There are no disincentives for going along with it. As we see, and why this thing hasn't finished yet, is because the people who went along with it are still the people who are in power

everywhere. We have an echo bubble going on now. Stock markets are ridiculously over-valued but all these people are saying 'it's wonderful' again. It's extraordinary, no one's been booted out of anywhere for pissing away billions of pounds.

And that was the final bit of the Tony Dye morality tale. Those people who had done the wrong thing, in finance and politics, had not only survived, they had flourished. Politicians and regulators everywhere took the hear no evil, see no evil, route and pinned it on the financiers. The financiers blamed it on governments, economists and everyone else. Barely anyone in finance responsible for the crash, in either the US or UK, was prosecuted. Some took a hammering in the media. But even people like Fred Goodwin, Adam Applegarth and Andy Hornby,[11] who lost their banks tens of billions, walked away with generous personal pension pots and new business positions.

Conclusion

Powerful, highly educated people, who head big companies, financial institutions and government departments are far less in control than we think. They lack specialist knowledge and big new ideas. They are reluctant to step out and do something markedly different. They follow more than they lead. Their personal incentives and sense of risk can run directly counter to those of their companies or wider society. This becomes all too apparent in times of crisis when the sense of personal risk becomes acute. And personal risk is reduced by running with the herd.

Herding not only increases the chances of survival; it means the trappings of leadership can be retained. It also means that leaders get to keep their professional legitimacy, networks and options open. They can stay or, if things begin to look bleak, they can quickly move on. Thus they remain mobile. And mobility takes us on to the next chapter.

Notes

1 For a wider account of how views of risk change society, see Ulrich Beck (1992) *Risk Society*, London: Sage.

2 See Ownership Commission (2012) *Plurality, Stewardship and Engagement*, London: Ownership Commission.

3 See J.M. Keynes (1936) *The General Theory of Employment, Interest and Money*, New York: Harcourt Brace and Co.

4 Some good insider accounts of events at Westminster are in: Anthony Seldon (2005) *Blair*, London: Free Press; Clare Short (2005) *An Honourable Deception? New Labour, Iraq and the Misuse of Power*, London: Free Press; and John Kampfner (2004) *Blair's Wars*, London: Free Press.

5 WMD: Weapons of Mass Destruction.

6 See Justin Lewis's study (2004) 'Television, Public Opinion and the War in Iraq: The Case of Britain' in *International Journal of Public Opinion Research*, Vol. 16, No. 3, pp. 295–310.

7 See Robert Schiller (2001) *Irrational Exuberance*, New Jersey: Princeton University Press.

8 See John Cassidy (2002) *Dot.Con: The Greatest Story Ever Told*, London: Penguin/Allen.

9 See figures in Vince Cable (2009) *The Storm*, London: Atlantic Books.

10 Tony Dye died in 2008 but saw the beginnings of the next financial crash he had also predicted. Once again, he was a bit too premature.

11 Fred Goodwin was CEO of the Royal Bank of Scotland 2001–9 and lost £24 billion in 2008 alone. Adam Applegarth was CEO of Northern Rock when it collapsed. Andy Hornby was CEO of HBOS when it needed to be publicly bailed out to the tune of £20.5 billion.

9 Liquid leaders and networks

Introduction

Many of the sources of modern-day elite power have changed. Leaders don't all have exclusive educations, stockpiles of money, established old-boys' clubs and secure jobs. But they do possess alternative resources: secrecy and invisibility, access to expert knowledge, connections with new flexible networks and, above all, mobility. In fact, in our globalised, unstable world, mobility has become 'the principle tool of power and domination'.[1]

For ordinary souls, mobility is associated with insecurity and precarity, but for elites, it can become a valuable commodity. Mobility means lack of past accountability. Those in charge can keep deferring tough decisions and expensive problems to their unfortunate successors. They can sacrifice all sorts of things for a result, then exit before the bankruptcy hits the fan.

Mobility also means future opportunity, enabling leaders to move quickly on to the next post, occupation or country as conditions change. Pension funds or the oil business today; hedge funds or hi-tech companies tomorrow. A civil service mandarin or minister to begin; a Harvard professorship and multiple executive board positions to finish. And sometimes, all these things at once. Why choose to be either a poacher or a gamekeeper when you can be both?

Lastly, mobility offers the possibility of leaders leveraging their assets – their contacts, knowledge and wealth. Money and homes can be spread across multiple nations. Legal and taxation systems can be exchanged when required. Wealth extracted from one unstable nation can be safely parked in a second state, and all of it registered in a third tax haven elsewhere.

Kicking the cans (and making them too)

For leaders, can-kicking is a regular temptation. All the more so if they have short-term tenures and get to be co-creators of their own appraisal system. Kicking the can traditionally entails ignoring looming problems, or aiming to make short-term gains rather than long-term investments. But these days, it can also involve something rather worse. That is, deliberately mortgaging the future to achieve a quick win now. In other words, leaders no longer just put off problems. Some have become adept at creating them for the next generation too.

In the business world, no-one admits that they do such things. But they assume others do. Short-term pressures are ever present. As James Hill, CEO of the Findus Group, put it: 'When I was younger, it was all about the long term. What I think I've learned is that, well, we're all dead in the long term … if it doesn't work straightaway, you're in deep trouble.'

It was Samir Brikho of AMEC who spelled out the temptations of CEOs most clearly. Brikho, having been at the company for eight years, evidently hadn't been playing the smash-and-grab leadership game himself. But when we talked, he seemed particularly sensitive to the pressures and where that was leading (he himself left not long after we had talked):

> you read that the average CEO tenure in businesses is becoming three years now. And if that's the case, it's bad news for the industry to be honest. And I'll tell you why. Because everybody can make much more money if you cut down on the R&D. If you don't spend it on the R&D then you can convert that to profit. That's great if you are there only two or three years but do you kill the company maybe later on? … So, if I'd been optimising only for the first two years in order to make the big buck at the third year, and then 'thank you very much and bye', that would be not great for the company's future … Because you could come. You could say: 'I don't need to do this. I don't need to do that.' You get the profit. I get my bonuses and then I go. And then the next CEO will suffer.

Clearly such temptations had proved too much for Sir Fred Goodwin and Dick Fuld, who bankrupted RBS and Lehman Brothers respectively. And, so too, for Sir Philip Green, who quietly extracted hundreds of millions from BHS, before selling it for a pound with debts of £1.3 billion. All of these captains of industry had previously been highly regarded across the business and political worlds. Each had won various business awards and honours when on the way up.

CEOs and financiers may bring down companies but politicians and civil servants can bring down whole nations. Ministers and mandarins have even shorter tenures and are equally adept at gaming their systems.

One particular interview made things frighteningly clear to me. This was with a very senior Treasury official. Since he can't be named, I will call him Blofeld. At the start of the conversation he spoke with a certain caution. Later, the conversation moved on to discussing PFI[2] contracts and the potential debts building up in the future. He smiled and responded as if this was a relatively small consideration: 'I don't have the figures to hand but in the scale of government capital spending PFI has never been huge frankly. It's never been big in the sort of fiscal arithmetic.'

Pushed about the then more than £300 billion of debt that were building up,[3] he replied with a dismissive wave of the hand: 'I doubt it was hundreds of billions. But, you know, we have a national debt into the trillions. So?' Noticing that his answer was not being fully appreciated, he tried to justify his statement:

> Look, if you're a government, you want to have more things. You want to announce you're going to open new schools and hospitals and so on. And, if you can find a way of doing that off-balance-sheet, that's quite convenient ... if you look at it in the scale of government capital spending, then the numbers are actually quite small ... In my experience governments generally want economies to grow by whatever means and in whatever places.

A year or two after that interview, Blofeld had moved on, taking some highly paid position in the private sector. It's hard to say what was more concerning; that he didn't actually know the scale of the debt being built up, or that he thought hundreds of billions was a negligible amount. But, either way, it wasn't going to be his problem anymore.

PFI is only one area where successive governments, left and right, have been creating cans to kick down the road. The privatisation of state industries and assets, begun in the 1980s, was not simply an ideologically driven policy. Nor was Mrs Thatcher's right-to-buy legislation for council housing simply about bribing the electorate. Both moves were also driven by governments desperate for additional income who wanted to offset the growing balance of trade deficits building up. Both policy pathways have continued, causing other public debts to rise as well as creating a major housing crisis.[4] Something similar has been happening with the new student loan system brought into higher education by the coalition government.[5]

But the biggest cans being kicked down the road all relate to the environment: food production, loss of biodiversity, water security, pollution, waste, deforestation, anti-biotic resistance and, of course, global warming.[6]

Working the public-private network

In classic studies of elites in the past, formal board networks were deemed to hold a key role in linking leaders across business.[7] An 'inner circle', or elite of the business elite, sat on a number of executive boards and provided a powerful tool of influence. For various reasons, such networks came to be seen as either irrelevant or outdated.

However, elite networks haven't disappeared. Rather, they have morphed into something more sophisticated and flexible. As authors such as the US anthropologist Janine Wedel have noted, higher-level leaders are no longer restricted to single organisations and professional sectors.[8] These 'flexians', as she calls them, move around mobile, fluid 'flex nets'. These networks straddle both public and private sector institutions, as well as operating through intermediary organisations like think tanks and consultancies.

For example, the same army general may advise a senate committee, sit on the board of a military contractor, and be a media commentator. He can then promote armed intervention, which requires billions being spent on private defence contracts for the same firm he is on the board of. An investment banker or top accountant may be seconded to advise government on new financial regulations or tax regimes. She can then return to advise corporate clients on how to adapt to or avoid the new regimes.

Such mobility and flexibility means that modern elites can exploit their insider knowledge across multiple organisations and occupations. It also enables them to leap from one sinking institution or sector to another.

Talking to top CEOs and former mandarins in the same period, it became apparent that several did move back and forth between public and private-sector networks. Every retired permanent secretary interviewed had since taken up a position on one or more corporate boards; sometimes while retaining a department advisory position too. The last five Treasury Permanent Secretaries (Lord Macpherson, Lord O'Donnell, Lord Turnbull, Lord Burns and Sir Peter Middleton) have all had periods, before and/or after, working in international finance (the IMF, World Bank, investment banks).

Lord Terry Burns has been a successful flexian for decades. A former colleague referred to him as 'a great networker', and put their invitation to work with the new Thatcher government down to Burns' skills here. The Labour minister Geoffrey Robinson, part of Gordon Brown's inner circle, described how Burns did something similar with New Labour in advance of their 1997 victory: 'the link with the Treasury was established a good year before, and the link man on our side was Ed Balls, and the man on their side was Terry Burns … Ed was seeing him every month.'

Burns continued to use those skills after he was eased out from his position as Permanent Secretary at the Treasury in 1998. Since then, he has had stints at Pearson, Legal and General, British Land, Glas Cymru, Marks and Spencer and Santander. He has also had similar roles at the National Institute of Economic and Social Research, the Royal Academy of Music, the National Lottery Commission, and has chaired several government inquiries and reviews.

In this respect, Blofeld, the off-balance sheet king in the Treasury, has also been an adept flexian. Before, during and since his stints in the civil service, he has been an executive or board member in several investment banks and FTSE 100 companies, as well as holding similar positions in public institutions.

Talking to captains of industry revealed that some were keen to develop their networks far beyond their own business sectors.[9] Sir Michael Davis of the Xstrata multinational mining company, set out his aims clearly:

> you should be talking to your peer group right across the stage internationally, locally or whatever. Other heads of organisations, not only mining companies. Bankers, retailers or whatever … A chief executive of a FTSE 100 organisation can meet whoever he wants to meet. You get invited to lunches, you go to dinners, you speak at

conferences, and you build up a network. As you build your network up, the value of a network is working that network.

And for these wider business networkers, the links spread across government too. They came into frequent contact with ministers, civil servants and regulators. This would be for direct lobbying or regulator negotiations but also as invited contributors for government task forces or policy discussion forums. Sir Ian Cheshire of B&Q, who seemed to know anyone and everyone, described his multiple networks, including those with government:

> There's one rather extraordinary thing which is newer, non-execs in government departments. And there's the lead non-execs, because I do work for the Department of Work and Pensions. And that is an extraordinary network of very senior business people who are interested in government, who meet quarterly, which Lord Browne organises.

Cheshire was describing a relatively new development. In recent years, Lord Browne, who previously led BP, began setting up corporate-style executive boards for each government department. 68 NEDs[10] were recruited from the private sector on to these, including 14 lead department NEDs.[11]

In many respects, this is just the latest, more formal step in the process by which the corporate and financial sectors have been colonising government management systems. By 2015, government departments were spending £800 million a year on outside consultants. The same has been true with the importing of corporate-sector management practices, and the marketisation of the NHS[12] and other state services.

In general, the revolving door between public and private-sector networks has increased steadily since the 1980s.[13] In the period 2010 to 2014 alone, some 600 former ministers and civil servants were appointed to business roles. And the UK's poorly regulated commercial lobby industry, smaller only than that of Washington and Brussels, has slowly spread its networks across Westminster and Whitehall.

Connecting the networks

The advance of these revolving doors and flex nets has, in part, been facilitated by the expansion of key intermediary professions.

Big organisations, as well as the super-rich, all employ experts in finance, accounting, law, business, public affairs and public relations. In many cases, just a handful of firms dominate each sector, servicing public and private institutions and individuals.

I got my first insight into how such intermediaries link disparate elite sectors when looking at the public relations profession in the 1990s. Then, the top three companies were Shandwick, Lowe-Bell and Dewe-Rogerson. All three simultaneously worked closely with the Conservative Party, were awarded regular Conservative government contracts and, between them, serviced over half the companies in the FTSE 100.

I interviewed Lord Tim Bell, who had worked for Saatchi and Saatchi when they assisted Mrs Thatcher's Conservative Party election campaigns. He later set up Lowe-Bell. For three decades, he juggled being Mrs Thatcher's favourite advisor with running an expanding corporate PR and lobbying agency that worked for anyone and everyone (including a variety of dictators and scandal-riven corporations). Bell spoke candidly about his knowledge of the networks that aided his objectives:

> And then there is the grapevine network. Politics is a very tiny place … if you know 100 people in the right places, you can talk to the whole country … There's a clear network and it's been speeded up by New Labour's unofficial consultation process. They talk about consultation now over new ideas and proposals but much of that consultation is simply unofficial stuff going on through the grapevine … The vast majority of policy decisions are taken by vested interests.

More recently, I was reminded of the roles played by professional intermediaries when speaking to top CEOs. During the conversations, it became clear that various consultants did more than just offer them expert advice. Financiers, head hunters, accountancy firms and business consultants also arranged regular networking events. As Warren East of ARM explained:

> I could go out to dinner in London every night of the week at some event or other … Organised by consultants who are generally either sort of trying to sell something to government or they've sold something. And so, there's a sort of governmenty slant on it. Or head-hunters or finance intermediaries.

Quite separately, I talked to Sir Ian Powell, who was Chairman and Senior Partner for eight years at PwC (PricewaterhouseCoopers), the largest accountancy firm in the UK and one of the 'big four' that dominate the profession globally. During the conversation, it transpired that Powell was one of those consultants who brought CEOs and others together on a regular basis: 'We use our firm to convene as well. So, once a month, I do a Chairman Senior Partner dinner, a private dinner, probably with about 20 to 25 business leaders, politicians, regulators. We have direct engagement with government. We have direct engagement with charities. So with all the stakeholders.'

As Powell talked, it became clear how knowledge, power and networks fused together. He used the word network several times. Management was organised through 'the network leadership team', and clients were connected to the firm through: 'PwC Spark, which is our own social and business network.' These networks were all about accumulating and using different sources of expert knowledge:

> We've got more people and more clients than anybody else. Therefore, if you aggregate it, we've got more knowledge. So the question is: have you got the procedures, systems, attitudes to share that knowledge and access that knowledge quickly? And the good news is the systems that we've invested in over the years, and the new social networking systems that are available, make it much, much easier to share and access that knowledge than it's ever been before.

At the time, it all sounded so positive: dynamic, forward-thinking, cooperative. PwC was the centre of a hive-like network linking the collective. But from another point of view, it also offered an insight into how such networks and expert knowledge combine to support the modern power elite and their flex nets.

And it works exceptionally well in relation to the big four accounting firms. These firms offer tax and management consultancy services to organisations, while also auditing them. In the UK in 2015, the big four audited the accounts of 96% of the FTSE top 350 companies. 46 of the finance directors of the FTSE 100 and 5 of the 15 members of the Financial Reporting Council previously worked at one of the big four.[14]

They are also present at all the main political party annual conferences and make financial contributions to each of them too.

Staff are regularly 'seconded' to work in the Treasury and HMRC as well as in the offices of senior politicians.[15] Over an 18-month period in the lead up to the 2015 election, PwC seconded staff worth £540,000 to Labour MPs, most prominently Ed Balls and Chuka Umunna. PwC is also a regular recruiter of former officials and ministers.[16]

And none of the big four, despite being frequently connected to tax evasion, fraud and money-laundering scandals, are ever substantially punished or investigated. They have become simply too big and too connected to discipline.

Leveraging the international assets

For some decades, globalisation has been promoted as a positive force by elites everywhere. But globalisation, whatever its wider positives and negatives,[17] has turned out to be extremely beneficial to elites themselves. International financiers, multi-nationals and the super-rich have all benefitted. The number of UHNWIs[18] and billionaires continues to climb annually. In 2010 the richest 388 people in the world had as much wealth as the bottom 50% of the global population. By 2016 just 8 people did.[19]

Those that have gained most are also those that are most mobile and able to take advantage of global communications, transport and international networks. So, large corporations and the super-rich spread their assets and homes across several nations, and plutocrats traverse international waters in their super yachts. In 2010, 83% of large companies had off-shore accounts and an estimated $21 trillion was held in such tax havens.

And London is just such a hub, reinvented and reshaped to accommodate its 80 plus billionaires and half a million UHNWIs. The capital is one of the world's top three financial centres. It is ably supported by specialist accountants and lawyers, and is one of the easiest jurisdictions for international investors to do takeovers, trade shares, and buy and sell property.[20] 54% of company shares traded in 2014 were foreign owned. 98% of FTSE 100 companies have subsidiaries or joint ventures registered in overseas tax havens. 60% of top-end homes in London were foreign-owned in 2012, 90% of which were bought and sold anonymously through tax havens.[21] And, the theatre and fine dining aren't bad either.

Most FTSE 100 CEOs have London offices but are also part of the global elite. More than a third are not UK-born. Several I met sounded very much connected into a series of international networks. They criss-crossed the planet frequently, surveying their company subsidiaries. They spoke to government ministers and their peers wherever they went. They did big deals and pushed through bigger takeovers worth billions.

They dropped in on the World Economic Forum in Davos and other exclusive leader events. They were as used to reading the *South China Morning Post* and *Harvard Business Journal* as they were the *FT*. They plugged into CNN, Bloomberg, Sky and the BBC. And all of them knew how to leverage their international networks and assets.

The person who epitomised all this for me was Sir Martin Sorrell, who made his initial reputation as Group Finance Director at Saatchi and Saatchi. Then, in 1985 he bought a small basket manufacturing company called Wire and Plastic Products. Using this shell, he began buying up advertising companies. Numerous takeovers later he had created the global advertising, PR and lobbying giant WPP. Its hundreds of subsidiaries, including big household names such as Hill and Knowlton, Young and Rubicam, and Ogilvy, employ over 200,000 people world-wide.

All of which was quite surprising as I approached WPP's tiny headquarters, tucked away in a side alley near Green Park. The waiting area, with its wall plastered with the logos of WPP's many subsidiaries, was the only thing to remind one that this was a global multi-national company. Sorrell himself appeared the true cosmopolitan. He spent only a third of his time in the UK. He compared his favourite media in New York and London. He gave the impression of someone always in meetings, always on the move, and always working his international networks:

> Clients I go and see. And stakeholders, most of them I go and see. Internally I go and visit our offices. We're in 110 countries. I go to certain conferences each year, the World Economic Forum, Allen & Company in the Sun Valley, Google's Zeitgeist, WPP Stream, Burning Man ... Going to the Singapore Summit next weekend.

Sorrell, unusually for a FTSE 100 chief, had led his company for three decades. But, even so, he was aware of the precarity of business and national economies. On chief executives, he remarked 'if you're a CMO in America you might last two years.' On new companies and industries, he offered: 'you can be disintermediated in a nano-second.' And on national economies:

> as we know from recent events, or possible future events, there's a limited amount that governments can do ... just like companies ebb and flow, countries ebb and flow, regions ebb and flow, and I think it's part of that. So, I think there's an inevitability about it which is very difficult. I think you have to go with the flow. You have to spot where the growth is.

Sorrell was fascinated with the changing tectonic plates of the global economy. In the different nations he has businesses in, he keeps tabs on the state of their infrastructure, tax and regulatory regimes, educational standards and several other things besides. Most of all, Sorrell has an idea of 'where the growth is', such as 'in the BRICs and Next 11'.[22] And Sorrell makes regular published forecasts on where things are going globally. Because where economies are growing, so is advertising. But whether he is right or wrong about a nation's prospects is not such an issue, because WPP has spread itself far beyond any single region. As he said: 'in WPP, every day I wake up and there's something good that happens and something bad that happens, and if you have 178,000 people in 110 countries, the odds are something's going to go wrong.'

Some things about Sorrell and WPP didn't make sense. He seemed as concerned as every other leader about all the 'unknown unknowns' out there. He was aware that things could change fast, economies dive, and CEOs be ejected. His tiny, barely visible offices did not seem to be the nerve centre of a global multi-national firm.

But things made more sense in other ways. Sorrell was, above all, an expert finance man and global networker, who was both spreading his risks, and exploiting the holes and differences of the international system. Scratch the surface and WPP looks like more of a shell holding company for its hundreds of actual businesses. Failing subsidiaries and regional operations can be ditched quickly if things go wrong; and new ones added if they are going right.

And WPP and Sorrell know how to exploit the financial networks of the world. WPP is a serial tax-avoider, usually paying no more than a few million annually on its hundreds of millions in stated profits. In a 2013 study of FTSE 100 companies, WPP came at the top in terms of the amount of offshore accounts it had: 618 in all.[23] But while appearing to make little profit in the UK, Sorrell can claim to make huge profits worldwide. Thus his personal annual pay and bonuses alone are considerably larger than WPP's UK tax bill. Since 2012 Sorrell's total pay has been £210 million, reaching £70 million in 2015 alone. In 2017, he was worth an estimated half a billion pounds.

Conclusion

In a remotely sane world, neither Boris Johnson nor Michael Gove would be in charge of anything, let alone major departments of state. Neither would the top bankers and CEOs who wrecked their banks and companies, nor the high-ranking officials and generals who have made disastrous economic and military decisions. But far too many of them are still there floating along at the top, seemingly immune and unashamed.

For all of them, mobility and networks have become key resources, allowing them to side-step the instabilities and breakdowns they have helped to produce. Canny leaders always have their escape plans ready, their assets and risks spread. They can deflect blame or defer responsibility. They can move organisation or sector, from public to private and back again. And, if things really look grim, they can rebalance their assets and relocate themselves to another country.

Unfortunately, ordinary corporations, nations and peoples are rather more immobile. They have no choice but to accept the consequences. They are left with greater insecurity and precariousness. And, in most cases, relocation options are very limited.

Notes

1 See Zygmunt Bauman (2007: 9) *Liquid Times: Living in an Age of Uncertainty*, Cambridge: Polity Press; and, more specifically, Thomas Birtchnell and Javier Caletrio's (2014) edited collection *Elite Mobilities*, Abingdon, Oxon: Routledge.

2 PFI: Private Finance Initiative.
3 From 1992, when the Major government began funding projects using PFI, to 2012, contracts with capital costs of almost £55 billion have been built. These have accrued long-term debts of £301 billion off-balance sheet to do this. See https://www.theguardian.com/news/datablog/2012/jul/05/pfi-contracts-list.
4 See James Meek (2014) *Private Island*, London: Verso; and, in relation to housing, Danny Dorling (2014) *All That is Solid*, London: Penguin.
5 See Andrew McGettigan (2013) *The Great University Gamble: Money, Markets and the Future of Higher Education*, London: Pluto Press.
6 As just one good text, see Naomi Klein (2015) *This Changes Everything: Capitalism vs. the Climate*, London: Penguin.
7 See, for example, Mark Mizruchi (1982) *The American Corporate Network, 1904–1974*, Beverly Hills: Sage; and Michael Useem (1984) *The Inner Circle: Large Corporations and the Rise of Political Activity in the US and UK*, Oxford: Oxford University Press.
8 See Janine Wedel (2009) *Shadow Elite*, New York: Basic Books; or (2014) *Unaccountable*, New York: Pegasus Books.
9 See Aeron Davis (2017) 'Sustaining Corporate Class Consciousness Across the New Liquid Managerial Elite in Britain' in *British Journal of Sociology*, Vol. 68, No. 2, pp. 234–53.
10 NED: non-executive director.
11 See Stephen Wilks's (2015) report *The Revolving Door and the Corporate Colonisation of UK Politics*, London: High Pay.
12 See Colin Leys and Stewart Player (2011) *The Plot Against the NHS*, London: Merlin Books.
13 See Tamsin Cave and Andy Rowell (2014) *A Quiet Word*, London: Bodley Head.
14 See High Pay Centre (2015) *Cheques and the City*, London: High Pay Centre.
15 'Seconded' staff are not paid by the political institutions and parties they are seconded to. They appear to be a form of voluntary help, offered by expert firms. But, of course, the seconded staff can then return to their firms with expert, insider knowledge and contacts gained from those temporary placements.
16 See Stephen Wilks's (2015) report *The Revolving Door and the Corporate Colonisation of UK Politics*, London: High Pay.
17 See critical evaluations such as Joseph Stiglitz (2003) *Globalization and its Discontents*, London: Penguin.
18 UHNWIs: Ultra High Net Worth Individuals.
19 See Deborah Hardoon's (2017) Oxfam paper *An Economy for the 99%*, Oxford: Oxfam.
20 See details of the international financialisation of the UK economy in Aeron Davis and Catherine Walsh (2017) 'Distinguishing Financialization

from Neoliberalism' in *Theory, Culture and Society*, Vol. 34, No. 5–6, pp. 27–51.

21 For figures and general accounts of elite mobility see Chrystia Freeland (2012) *Plutocrats: The Rise of the New Global Super-Rich*, London: Penguin; or John Urry (2014) *Offshoring*, Cambridge: Polity Press.

22 Both terms refer to sets of emerging economies seen to have good future growth prospects. The BRICs are Brazil, Russia, India and China. The Next 11 are another set which includes Egypt, Indonesia, Mexico, South Korea, Nigeria and Indonesia.

23 See the *Guardian*'s Datablog at: https://www.theguardian.com/news/datablog/2013/may/12/ftse-100-use-tax-havens-full-list.

Conclusions

Solitary, rich, nasty, brutish and short[1]

Anyone who has read this far (and not just jumped to the end) will realise that this book isn't just meant to demonise and expose those in charge. Yes, I have met a few arsewipes over the years; some very rich and very self-serving arsewipes. But most of the elite figures I have talked to, even the highly paid ones, had a complex mixture of motivations and intentions. Many have made big personal sacrifices to serve some imagined higher purpose.

They also share many testing occupational conditions. Whether they are bankers or bureaucrats, correspondents or captains of industry, they experience related dilemmas, and have similar responses and behaviours. This leads to the wider point of the book, which is that the problems of leadership are as much related to the conditions, systems and practices in which elites now operate, as to the individuals themselves. So things can't be solved simply by doing away with the Boris Johnsons and Philip Greens of this world.

More than that, the 'ideal' leaders we like to imagine are not that common. Neither are they particularly likely to rise to the top in the current environments in which elites operate. Given that most actual leaders are less than exceptional, what is it about their working environments that encourage certain negative forms of conduct? To answer this, I have sought to draw out some of the more common themes that I have noticed appear and reappear through the book.

One of these is the increasingly technocratic and functional nature of leadership. So many leaders now appear to lack specific expertise, are not particularly innovative and creative, and do not offer new ideas and vision. Such issues do not particularly aid elites in their advance to the top. Networking and media skills, accounting knowledge and salespersonship do. Becoming an expert just slows a leader down, and expertise now has a limited shelf life. So they become reliant on other experts who are rarely neutral advisors.

Ideas and innovations are risky too, because they require bigger investments and take too long. They also make one stand out from the crowd. It's easier to copy others' ideas and what seems to work, than do something really new and different. Old ideas are easier to evaluate than new ones. Assessors without ideas of their own can hardly judge those who have them.

So leaders often follow rather than lead. Alternatively, they quietly replace ideas and grander plans with narrow, codable and verifiable targets. And, once the numbers games begin, time spans appear to get shorter. That which is difficult to quantify, like creativity and social well-being, becomes of marginal interest. And the mediocre leader replaces real innovation with a series of small movements on a ledger.

A second theme is the reshaping of elite cultural ties. New elites are more socially fragmented than before. Their collective identities, based on shared social class backgrounds, have declined. The links between money, power, education and social status have been broken. Since these things were originally used to define the Establishment, it's difficult to say it still exists.

Instead, elites have become more vaguely linked by key ideas, norms and practices. The tenets of neoliberalism and globalisation, loosely defined, have been widely accepted in most British leadership sectors. They all agree that states should be smaller, markets and trade freer, and individuals choosier and more calculating. They also draw on the same professions and practices which direct diverse elite environments. And, whether it is new technology, law, accounting or public relations, it is the same small set of dominant intermediary firms which guide them.

At the same time, ideas and practices do not necessarily bring social cohesion across dissimilar sets of leaders. In the insular spaces that elites inhabit, some very powerful ideas and fashions can form and be disseminated in a form of elitethink. But these may be starkly opposed to those generated in another elite sphere. And the Establishment divisions are now everywhere to see: in Brexit, the financial system, paralysed state bureaucracies, and in imploding mainstream parties.

So, too, the basic contradictions of neoliberalism itself are further fragmenting elites. Large corporations, markets and the super-rich depend on states to function; but their crippling of national institutions, in order to free such 'wealth creators', jeopardises the very systems they rely on. Equally, the focus on individualism, self-interest and harsh competition pushes each leader to put themselves above the Establishment collective.

That emphasis on individualism and self-interest in elite life is a third theme that repeats throughout the book. The precarity of leadership accentuates individualism at the top. It's clear that most modern organisational heads are acutely aware of the uncertainty of their position. The pressure on them to get results intensifies. They are encouraged to think and behave accordingly. Fear, as well as greed, drives those in the higher tiers. Thus personal risk is always weighed up against organisational or system risk. The higher the position, the bigger the stakes and the larger the risk. And personal risk often comes first.

That leads to a fourth theme central to elite existence: short-termism. Short-term results are balanced against long-term plans and investments. Those at the top know that they are likely to be pushed (if they don't jump first) sooner rather than later. If leadership has a limited lifespan then the short-term takes precedence. Sometimes the long-term is sacrificed altogether for the need to make a quick gain and justify a tenure. There is rarely a penalty for those failures that only come to light a year or two after an organisational head has departed.

Mobility and transience are a fifth theme. Whether it's a choice they make, or one that is forced upon them, elites have become exceedingly mobile. They move jobs, careers and national jurisdictions. Some hedge their occupational bets and skirt across several sectors at once. They glide across exclusive networks, making temporary stops as required.

All this means they have weak personal relations with those around them. They have little attachment to organisations or communities or nations. They have no substantial stake or enduring responsibility for any of these things. Why make real friends or long-term commitments when you are always about to move on? Psychologically and socially, as well as physically, they are detached nomads.

In effect, elite existence has become 'solitary, rich, nasty, brutish and short.'

Systems and principles for reining in the elite

We are long overdue an overhaul of many of our systems and institutions. So many have become something they were never intended to be. Yet leaders and the public continue as if they still operate as they once did. Progressive change in all of them would certainly rein in leaders and re-attach them to publics in various ways.

It would be arrogant and naive to suggest I can offer system-type solutions to the grander problems that elites have caused in Britain (and many similar nations) – from deindustrialisation to financialisation, extreme inequality to environmental catastrophe, the mess of the Middle East to the bodge of Brexit, political paralysis to property market dysfunction. On all these things, much has already been written by specialists and reformers in the five sectors I have discussed. They have weighed up alternatives and made detailed suggestions for improved systems. They are in many of the publications cited in this book, as well as in many good academic and independently funded research centres and interest groups (but not often in Westminster-based think tanks). As a quick summary:

In politics, our first-past-the post electoral system is not one that any emerging democracy would select now. The lack of a written constitution and poor set of checks and balances belong to an anachronistic past. Reform of our secretive, amateur and insular civil service was a necessary step; but simply marketising it and shifting its functions into the hands of unaccountable, often incompetent and insular private hands, has been regressive.

The City may appear to be a thriving, world-beating sector but it is a broken, destructive system. Behind the accounting façade it takes far more than it gives. It handicaps British industry and unbalances the economy. Financial market theory is nonsense. Opaque and exotic financial instruments don't spread risk; they destabilise finance and the real economy. There are many other nations that have more balanced, stable economies with smaller and more regulated financial sectors.

Likewise, systems of corporate governance, although an improvement on times past, are still pretty much a stitch-up between senior management and big investors. Shareholder value, the first and last law of governance, simply leads to no value for anyone or anything else. Again, there are lots of alternative models out there, both in the UK and abroad.

Our news media is equally broken and damaging. Democracy, markets and societies require shared public forums. But most news operations are not independent, autonomous, fourth estate services to society. They are the playthings of right-wing billionaires. Their business models have failed and the online world is no like-for-like replacement. We need a proper debate and rethink on how national news media are to be regulated and funded.

In each of these areas, there is always a tendency to centralise, develop powerful hierarchies of control, and exclude the local and bottom-up. State bureaucracies, global markets, political parties, news media and companies all seek efficiencies which cut out the local and the majority. It's not that publics want a greater say over every complex national policy issue, but they do want more input into the local institutions, public services, economies and companies that they are part of.

Those big intermediary professions, such as law, public affairs and accounting, need proper investigation, transparency and accountability too. They make elite networks tick. They are the physical proof of what pure money power can do and, accordingly, have become powerful generators of inequality in their own right. Increasingly, it is only the super-rich, large corporations and government institutions which can afford to employ these expert knowledge makers and keepers. And they frequently do so to become unaccountable, invisible, avoid taxes, and change laws and regulations to their benefit.

Perhaps more important than picking better systems and institutions is setting out the principles that guide any such overhauls, because elites, like everyone else, adapt to their systems and eventually push them out of their correct alignment. Thus the more democratic electoral systems of proportional representation are also throwing up extreme, self-interested and populist leaders. Traditional banks, which didn't have highly risky investment operations, were also brought down by the financial crisis. And billionaires have thrived in every political and economic system, including the far more equal Scandinavian nations.

So, in adapting and choosing systems that may produce more appropriate leaders, certain principles might be adopted and initiatives taken:

* **Transparency:** Elites resist this whenever possible. But so much more can be done with the will to enforce public transparency,

such as proper registering of lobbyists and party donations, publication of top organisational salaries and the ratio of highest to lowest paid staff, property ownership and financial accounts held abroad, and so on.

* **Conflicts of interest:** I am regularly amazed at how so many elite institutions exist with glaring conflicts of interest. Accountancy firms that both audit a company's accounts and sell tax advice to them. Investment banks which sell company shares while also flogging services to those same companies. Public affairs firms which fund all-party committees in Parliament. Media owners and editors who regularly meet senior party figures. Most of this should not happen and could simply be changed with legislation if the will was there.

* **Checks and balances:** Notions of accountability in democracies and markets look to checks and balances on elites to hold them to account. But, too often, the checks and balances are far too weak or non-existent. They are as assumed as much as real. Parliament is particularly unbalanced, especially when a Prime Minister has a strong majority. Select committees have little power over departments of state. Shareholders rarely work together to hold managements to account or challenge bloated CEO pay packages. They have limited powers of intervention anyway. Those elites who are supposed to hold other elites to account must be empowered to truly do so.

* **No self-policing:** I am also stunned by how many elite sectors get to regulate themselves. For years, the Press Complaints Commission was made up of only selected news people. IPSO is not much better. The ACOBA committee[2] that polices and advises ministers and civil servants taking up outside appointments is entirely inadequate. Every financial regulatory body and review is dominated by financial insiders. And every corporate executive board is full of friends and colleagues in the business world. All such major regulatory committees need more outsiders than insiders running them. Corporate boards need more non-corporate representatives, especially on their remuneration committees.

* **Sticks:** The failure to properly punish and deter elite crimes and failures is shocking. Repeatedly, too many banks and corporations are still fined in amounts that are a fraction of the gains made through illegal behaviour. Leaders are not held personally

accountable for large-scale failures, or prosecuted or put in jail for actions which lead to employee deaths and company collapses. Accountability structures, ones that operate in the longer-term for elites, including after their departure, need to be better developed.

* **... and carrots:** Probably, and there is some evidence to support this, bonus systems should be scrapped entirely. Why pay people more to do what they should be doing? But, if maintained, there needs to be much more thought about aligning incentives to the long-term interests of the organisation and its wider stakeholder base. Too often such systems are short-termist, numbers-based, easily gamed, and co-constructed by those being assessed. The prime examples are CEO bonuses linked to share price rises, and trader bonus structures in finance. There are many alternatives out there.

* **Neutral, public information:** Everywhere, the news and public information essential to markets, politics, choices and decisions has been left to market forces and so compromised. Most think tanks and many so called expert institutions are funded by and too close to political and big corporate interests. News and public reports are full of hidden non-neutral source material. Top legal information is only available to the few. There has to be some public reflection on this and a commitment to publicly funded sources of news, legal advice and detailed policy research and information.

* **Forget social mobility, it's inequality stupid!** For decades now, politicians of all sides have justified inequality and market forces on the basis that social mobility makes things fair. But such policies, mainly around education and welfare support, have obviously failed. As long as extreme inequality is sanctioned and markets given their head, mobility policies alone will always fail (something New Labour never worked out). More drastic action needs to be contemplated, including a return to active fiscal policies on everything from higher rate tax to property ownership and inheritance duties. Private schools and private health care providers should not have charity status. Pay can be capped, as much for premiership footballers and CEOs as for investment bankers.

* **More markets are not the only answer:** Publicly owned businesses, institutions and bureaucracies have many faults but so do private

ones. Certain services evidently work better, are more joined up and cost-effective in public hands. Many current market sectors would operate more efficiently and be more socially useful with greater public intervention. This isn't about adding tomes of new regulation or picking winners, it's about setting clear rules and boundaries. Currently, the financial market, housing market, and many utilities markets are very defective and exploitative. Governments don't have to run them but they can legislate and regulate to better direct these markets.

* **Culture and ethics are poor mechanisms:** Frequently, elites confronted with a failure suggest solutions around 'changing the culture' or new codes of ethics. They have all sorts of phrases for this, like corporate social responsibility or shareholder activism. They are just another way of saying elites can regulate themselves. They may increase awareness and change small things at the margins but, essentially, they are pretty useless, especially when they make no difference to the evaluation or pay of elites.

* **Reform the intermediary professions:** It is time that intermediary professions like public affairs lobbyists, accountants and certain parts of the legal profession were subjected to wide-ranging public enquiries. Their roles in facilitating corrupt practices and their contamination of political and economic processes has become endemic. They are at the heart of elite power and inequality.

* **Ideas and innovation:** I'm not sure how we might once again increase the proportion of leaders with imagination, expertise and vision, although dropping an increasingly test-based education system (for pupils and staff), as high-achieving nations like Finland have, would be a positive step. Vetoing PISA participation would also bring improvement. So might many of the suggested points above. Creativity and new approaches need time, nurturing and experimentation. Reforming the sticks and carrots regimes, the forms of checks and balances, etc. would all encourage these.

There are plenty of other ways. Leadership doesn't have to be solitary, rich, nasty, brutish and short. It can be connected, modestly paid, nice, civilised and long. And that would be pretty beneficial to everyone else too.

Notes

1 The original quote from Thomas Hobbes's *Leviathan* reads 'solitary, poor, nasty, brutish and short', and refers to the ungoverned masses rather than rulers.
2 IPSO: Independent Press Standards Organisation; ACOBA: Advisory Committee on Business Appointments.

Index